Pain, Purpose,
Passion

Pain, Purpose, Passion

That Was Then, This Is Now

Peter Ajello*Cindy Anderson*
Kathleen Booker*Sandra Champlain*
Joe Cirulli*Marilyn Gansel*
Erin Garcia*Cathleen Halloran*
Pamela Holtzman*Susan Jacobs*
Jason Jean*Betsy Jennings*
Margaret-Mary Kelly*Joe Leonardi*
Jeremy Manning*Mary Monahan*
Mel Morgan*Craig Piso*
Martin Plowman*Betty Ruddy*
Deanna Stull*Tessa Zimmerman

Compiled by Dr. Marilyn Gansel
Edited by Patricia G. Horan

The Round House Press
Asheville, North Carolina

The Round House Press
Asheville, North Carolina

ISBN: 978-0-9823089-7-4

Publisher's Cataloging-in-Publication Data
Gansel, Marilyn.
    Pain, purpose, passion : that was then, this is now / compiled
by Dr. Marilyn Gansel ; edited by Patricia G. Horan ; Peter
Ajello [and 21 others]. -- Asheville, North Carolina: The Round
House Press, [2015]
    pages ; cm.
    ISBN: 978-0-9823089-7-4
    Summary: Inspiring stories by twenty-two who journeyed from
devastation to revelation. What does it take to *more* than survive our stories, to more than merely overcome in the face of
what we fear most? Each of these true stories offers these gifts:
breathtaking candor, the kind of courage that lies hidden in all
of us, and a powerful glimpse of the same life-saving light we,
too, are seeking.--Publisher.
    1. Life change events--Personal narratives. 2. Change
(Psychology)--Personal narratives. 3. Survival--Personal narratives. 4. Addicts--Personal narratives. 5. Loss (Psychology)-
-Personal narratives. 6. Accidents--Personal narratives. 7. Be-
reavement--Personal narratives. 8. Encouragement. 9. Inspiration. 10. Courage. 11. Fortitude. 12. Conduct of life. I. Horan,
Patricia G. II. Ajello, Peter. III. Title.

BF637.L53 G36 2014	2014957297
155.9/3--dc23	1412

Cover design: Beth Shaw, Stormcloud Studio, Munich
Book design: raqoon-design.com
Printed in the United States of America

Loving ourselves through the process of owning our own stories is the bravest thing we'll ever do.

Brené Brown

Contents

Part Two
The Power of "Yes"

Part Three
Learning from Loss

Part Four
Mastership of Mind

Part Five
What the Tragedy Taught Me

EDITOR'S PREFACE

Fierce, often breathtaking candor. The drama of deep transformation. These twenty-two stories really don't need to offer anything else. But they do, many of them: They also let us in on the secret of what it takes to truly heal from the deepest, even the most tragic of life's experiences.

As Dr. Marilyn Gansel and I read each arriving story, we were profoundly struck by a sweet surprise in so many of them: the author's decision—conscious or not—to own the deep lesson he or she had learned, often by placing that painful experience in service to others facing similar challenges. (Marilyn, of course, is one of these authors herself, veteran of an undeniably abusive childhood who grew up intent on boosting the esteem of the most "impossible" students she taught, and who succeeds in doing so to this day as a life coach to the likes of me and so many others.)

She is in amazing company here.

What can you do to remain whole as a poor young girl after your perfect little baby boy is ripped from your arms "for your own good"? If you are carrying the alchemy of transformation, that is if you are Cindy Anderson, you become a midwife to other penniless young girls whose babies are similarly threatened. Simple, yes. Easy? No.

But that's the way they roll, our authors. Mel Morgan, for instance, healing after the trauma of losing a leg at a young age by consciously taking in the love and support of her family and her faith, and then starting an organization to support others facing a similar loss. There's Sandra Champlain, so intent on discovering what is tearing her family apart that she dives into researching a familiar culprit with the unrecognized power to literally rewire our brains: grief. And if, like Pamela Holtzman, you find yourself the only survivor from your cancer survivors' group, you head for hospice work on your way to starting your own healing center.

You will also be delighted and impressed, as Dr. Gansel and I have been, by the creative, original way these messages of hope and inspiration have been conveyed by their authors, such as the indomitable Joe Cirulli's conviction that he was building his "internal resume" during his most difficult struggles, despite what seemed like stark appearances to the contrary.

The inspired storytelling continues when Jason Jean describes himself as "serving a life sentence to things" before a near tragedy showed him what it really cost him to aggressively maintain his much-envied lifestyle. (And, like Betsy, Erin, and Susan, Jason admits he's ever-vigilant about possible relapse into old thinking.)

Holistic is good, right? Not if you're addicted to it. That's why we admire Susan Jacobs for being able to step outside her (much younger) self far enough to see that her dependence on healers had turned her into "my own mini-cult." We also love her Westernized take on the Eastern concept of "monkey mind"—she calls it "the CNN news crawl of thoughts." Got it.

Okay, but what could be bad about exercise? Ask Betsy Jennings, so addicted to it that she refused to travel without her trampoline, admitting that even today she can tell when she's headed back to compulsive exercising under stress—her walk will display secret telltale signs. Betsy has placed her consistent vigilance in service to her continued recovery, and—no surprise—she coaches others in the ways of freedom, as well.

On a personal note, I must cite Marilyn again, for a single sentence that I keep returning to for its troubling truth in my life: "Finally I finished the job... and shut myself down entirely." Frankly, I've never read anything that better described my own life as a profound stutterer from the age of nine, after the sudden, unexplained death—and perceived abandonment—of my beloved grandmother, my protector. Not only that, but working with these other powerful stories allowed me to realize that my own story belongs among them, something that hadn't occurred to me.

I realized for the first time that, like so many of our writers, I also intuitively chose a profession directly related to my greatest loss, my voice. I chose a craft that I long ago discovered can be a healing art. For what is my chosen role in life? Supporting others in being heard, by coaching writers and doing what I call "conscious editing," the work I love.

My own unexpected experience with these twenty-two personal accounts reinforced my belief that they can lighten each of our journeys if we take them to heart and apply them to our own unique challenges.

Betty Ruddy's stunning insight wakes her up to a life-changing revelation: The missing person in the FBI TV show she escapes into every week is Betty herself. And who but an Irish mystic would know to consciously carry along to her estranged sister's deathbed the transforming power of the raging storm that almost prevented her from being there? It should be no surprise that more than one miracle took place for Margaret-Mary Kelly that day.

Peter Ajello introduces us to the mind-blowing concept of weight-loss as an Olympic sport—where he's undeniably won the Gold as well as the attention of the media. Peter reveals one of his darkest secrets... chocolate.

Joe Leonardi, medical background and all, wonders how he allowed himself to become so dangerously addicted to carbs, sugar, and alcohol. In order to find out, he takes himself to a favorite childhood place of peace. Listening in the silence, he remembers a horrifying moment with a beloved grandmother who lost her mind and messed with his, a nightmare he's been hiding from, whether behind weight or musculature, ever since.

Kathleen Booker, meanwhile, with refreshing and courageous candor, lets us in on her prosperity crisis as well as her visceral response (ouch) to baring her soul on our pages, as she dares to dig deeper into her painful past than most people ever can or will. Her delicious interpretation of the Universe's call to action: "Kathleen, pick up your life!"

No, these are not ordinary stories.

"Because I thought I wasn't able to know everything, that I wasn't able to be 'perfect,' my only option was to fall apart." How's that for Tessa Zimmerman's chillingly perfect description of perfectionism?

Jeremy Manning, bottoming out and unable to feel self-love, uses his mother's death to finally receive the depth of her love for him, opening him up to his own ability to love himself in a powerful, skillfully observed moment: "Suddenly the nonsense of my retreat from the life my mother just lost stood up starkly, the way the ground seems to stand up when you fall."

Pamela Holtzman, after interrupting her top model's flawless life by coming frighteningly close to death, shares her hard-won conviction that "the work of dying is living fully." Martin Plowman comes to share that conviction, but only after being minutes away from death after a devastating racetrack crash, where he is introduced to fear and prayer, both for the very first time, while on a gurney struggling to breathe.

Craig Piso inadvertently validates all the stories in this book in his dual role of author/psychologist, "The recognition and acceptance of any truth, no matter how disturbing, is liberating and empowering." He shares more than one life-altering truth in his own dramatic story, including becoming able to forgive what most would describe as absolutely unforgivable treatment of a child. I urge readers not to miss the last three paragraphs of his story for a masterful description of the transformational process Craig has spent his personal and professional life observing from the inside.

Erin Garcia describes one of this culture's most baffling and dangerous afflictions—an eating disorder—with an unforgettable description of her own: "A silent cry, uttered in an effort to bring order to chaos, a cry my traumatized parents could not hear." Marilyn Gansel's troubling childhood memories are similarly poignant as she reminds us just how impossible it is to feel attractive when you are made to feel invisible.

A leading magazine can call you a beauty, another can call you "a sensation," and you can be a hit in the fussy fashion world, but when your horse stumbles on the dewy grass the way Christopher Reeve's did, your coma is no less real. Cathleen Halloran's design business had finally won the attention of *Vogue* and the other heavy hitters in her world. Then she went for that dewy morning ride. "I was the girl you would ask to get your cat out of the tree," she says in her candidly colorful fashion, "Now I need a shower chair. I fall over putting my underwear on and my morning coffee comes out my nose." Cathleen woke up laughing, and she makes sure that we do, too, as we marvel at her bulletproof gratitude.

A beloved mother's covert suicide attempts trouble her relationship with her daughter, Mary Monahan, until a fleeting moment of wordless healing at a hospice bedside is validated by a liberating message discovered in an abandoned closet. A brief piece of long-lasting poignancy.

Deanna Stull's final journey with her beloved Blake enables her to offer us eleven powerful insights to guide us in living our own lives, and in one of them she inadvertently describes exactly what she and our other authors have done in writing their stories:

"Let's spend the majority of our time here doing things we'd like to be known for, instead of things that are easy to cross off a list," Deanna suggests. Check!

Here are life lessons so universal that as we read these stories we realize we are seeing their themes acted out around us all the time. Betsy Jennings' addiction to everyday exercise was so serious that it easily could have killed or maimed her. Her graphic insight into what lay at the root of her addiction is chillingly familiar:

"I lived a life totally devoted to purging an imaginary internal poison."

If we are honest in describing our response to the cruel demands of this culture, who among us has not felt at least a fleeting attraction to that deadly distortion?

Joe Cirulli takes us to "One day when I found myself sitting in someone's office and opened a drawer...

and started reading about people who faced multiple challenges and overcame them, accomplishing extraordinary things simply by changing the way they thought, setting goals and meeting them. This was the beginning of a whole new world for me, a world built on the inspiring stories of others who had accomplished extraordinary things while working through the worst of circumstances." It's more than likely that one day, during a challenging time, somebody else will open a drawer and lift out this book, and Joe's will be a story that changed a life.

What a lovely legacy.

Patricia G. Horan

Introduction

My Reason for Gathering and Sharing These Stories

Dr. Marilyn Gansel

"There is no greater agony than bearing an untold story inside you," said Maya Angelou.

We all have heartbreaking stories. No matter who we are, what career we chose, what societal class we are blessed or cursed to be identified with, we all have some level of worry, anguish, and distress in our histories, along with our precious moments of joy, self-discovery and compassion.

As I read the stories our writers have entrusted to me, they not only brought home the truth that we truly are not alone, they also made it clear to me that unless we *share* our soul-inspiring stories, we risk remaining silently stuck in our pain.

I know first-hand how it feels to endure in silence, voiceless, outwardly stoic, and emotionally dying inside. For some time I knew I had my own story to share, but I didn't know where or how to do that. And, I wondered, who would want to know my story, anyway? Would anyone relate to it? Would anyone care?

1

I know now that each chapter of my narrative can either enhance, transform, or destroy me or the people around me. I can also take each event in my life, especially the painful incidents, and with them I can design a new story. I know we have the ability—the resilience—to turn the impossible to possible, even though so many of the stories that shaped us early in life are not ones we think we'd have chosen to experience.

We have the power to turn *pain* into *purpose* and then into *passion*, and this book is full of the stories that prove it.

I had first come upon the idea to collaborate on a series of short stories about pain, purpose, and passion after more closely examining my own life story, my own painful growing-up experiences of being unwanted, rejected before my life had even really begun. As I look back on all the events that were both the causes and effects of non-acceptance, I realized that, while I had moments of "happiness," even joy, those moments were covered by layers of shame, guilt, and utter sadness. I suffered from anxiety (still do today) and depression. I was labelled a "slow learner" as a child, and built my story around what I was told and what I believed to be true then.

It wasn't till my teens and college years that I began to question authority, my beliefs and values, to better understand who I was. I needed to know why I had to feel such pain. Was I a bad person? Was this my destiny? When things around me turned ugly or sour, would I choose life or death? And what was it about my experience of rejection that caused me to *attract* the abandoned, the lost, and the hopeless people? I believe my rejection was a *gift* I was given, so that I would be more likely to compassionately and unconditionally love the students, friends, and strangers I met during each chapter of my life, to allow me to understand their feelings, their pain, and agony. I knew how they felt when told they would not amount to anything. *I had been them.*

The chapters of my life had formed a world, around which I found purpose and then, suddenly, passion.

I began to realize there are others like me who made it a practice to see opportunities for change, despite such dire circumstances as financial failure, the death of a loved one, a debilitating illness, a devastating injury, a tormenting addiction. It's as if they rewired their thinking and re-evaluated their self-worth, determined not to let circumstances rule. Subsequently, their pain morphed into their purpose, which in turn became their passion. And, in the end, their journey from devastation to revelation became their healing instrument.

Once I thought I suffered alone, that I was the only person going through difficulties, so I plodded along, not voicing how I felt. Quite honestly, there were many times I didn't know what or how to feel. I only knew I felt conflicted. But then, as I began attracting people like me, I realized I was not alone. *We* are not alone. We can lift each other up. We can help each other find a reason for the pain, then turn that hurt into a reason for living and giving back. We can find our true purpose. As Maya Angelou so dramatically put it, we need to share our story, or the agony of the untold tale consumes us; we drown in our suffering, while our silence can offer no hope for others like us.

I started understanding other people's pain to an even greater degree after earning my doctorate in Applied Sports Psychology. I became a life coach, offering personal and group coaching, when I was given the opportunity to host my own Internet radio show for two years. My program, *What's Weighing You Down?* became a vehicle for me to meet the most amazing individuals, people whose stories powerfully affected me. Many of those who were on my show are now the contributing authors for this, our series' first book.

I want to thank all our authors for their patience while we published this first book, and for their incredible bravery in sharing and gifting the world with stories of hope and inspiration. Many of them told me that after sharing their stories they felt enormous relief and healing.

I want to thank my wonderful, kind, and talented publisher, Patricia Horan of The Round House Press, for believing in this project and for her impeccable editing guidance. Her intuitive suggestions throughout this process have been spot-on!

I also want to thank my dear husband, Robert, for his love and support in all my endeavors—you are so loved!

And to all our readers, may you be filled with love, hope, joy, and peace. Know always that you can be triumphant, that your pain, when told, can offer you purpose and passion. Look for it. Then share it.

Part One

Hooked on More... or Less

Mind Over Body—
All 445 Lbs of It

Peter Ajello

"Sometimes a weight-loss story just simply breaks through new barriers. If weight loss was an Olympic sport, then Peter Ajello would certainly be a contender for a gold medal."

This is just one of the story leads written about me that I am so grateful for. You see, I lost 200 pounds in sixteen months and made my mark on the world, proving that obesity, heart disease, diabetes, addictions, and depression *can* be overcome without surgery or medication. It was such an incredible feat that I still have to look twice in the mirror to make sure this is reality!

At the onset, I was so overweight that my life was in serious danger. At my maximum, I had reached 445 pounds. I was suffering from diabetes, had dangerously high cholesterol levels, and was tormented by gout attacks that literally disabled me. I was morbidly obese and quite possibly had less than a year to live. I was on fourteen different medications for the problems caused by my obesity.

Fat was no longer funny
And then there was the inevitable wakeup call. I suffered a near-fatal diabetic stroke after a usual day of bingeing on fried foods and sugar-laced cocktails. That was it. I had to face the fact that being obese was not acceptable, neither was it funny. I was about to begin the battle of my life against addiction and a severely dysfunctional relationship with food.

First I had to dig deep inside me and do the requisite soul searching in order to find out just how I had gotten where I was in the first place. To start,

I know my parents' divorce when I was a thirteen-year-old had initiated my love of comfort foods. The raging arguments that ensued and my subsequent move to Florida with my father, away from all I knew and all my friends, fueled my desire to eat with reckless abandon. Doughnuts, fast food, and buttery corn muffins—they all filled the void now permanently residing within me.

To top it all off, I was now a free agent. No rules, no supervision, and no guidance. This opened the door to wild activities and mischief, up to and including my abuse of drugs and alcohol. I was even somewhat proud of my new endeavors. I liked being "Fat Pete," the one who held over-the-top parties and supplied the best drugs in town.

My perilous descent continued right through college and beyond, until that one fateful day when I awoke, face slanted, bloodied nose, and unable to speak properly. After a trip to the ER and a serious scolding from my doctor, I knew I had to change, but had no concept of the work and commitment that it would take. Thanks to many kind people and the grace of God, I received the necessary support and direction I needed to go into battle, fully armed and ready to fight.

I won the battle by first enduring eleven days of sheer hell as I detoxed from drugs. I must have been a disastrous sight, detoxing at 445 pounds, but it was the necessary preliminary step that made the rest possible. I will never forget my father dragging me to the shower up to ten times a day in response to my alternating moments of shivering freezes and bed-soaking sweats.

Just when I thought I could not go on any longer, my actor friend Mike Byron called from the set of *Shutter Island*, where he was working with Leo Di-Caprio. He said to me, "Peeta- you got this, *you can do it*, TOUGH TIMES PASS, TOUGH PEOPLE STICK!" And with that I fell into a half-sleep that carried me through to a new day, a day when I finally felt that a massive elephant had finally jumped off my back. Shortly thereafter, I received a signed picture of my friend Mike, on the set with Leo. I was so grateful for that call and my new souvenir!

My friends were betting... against me
Inspired by my success, I next moved on to my diet, or lack thereof. I modified my diet from drive-throughs to home-cooked, high-fiber, low-glycemic meals. Another major tool in my success was organic dark chocolate. This indulgent treat, a strong antioxidant, was a mainstay in my daily routine. So was exercise, whether it was strength training, spinning classes, or simply walking—the only thing possible for me to do early on.

I also had another strong motivational factor lighting the fire inside me: a $17,000 bet waged in 2009 by my close friends, betting that I *could not* lose 150 pounds by the New Year. Though I was clear that I was embarking upon my new life as a matter of life or death—mine!—I must admit that this wager sure made my journey more interesting. Anyone who knows me knows I'm a betting man, and this time I was betting on myself to win.

What followed was six intense months, marked by my determination not to fail. I did whatever it took to keep that number on the scale moving down. I started with organic weight-loss cookies. That jump-started my weight loss nicely, albeit not healthfully. With my friend Google and some advice from a local fitness trainer and nutritionist, I continued to modify my diet to include the aforementioned fibrous foods. I stocked up on vegetables, fruit, and organic chocolate.

No one was stopping me now.

Next would come exercise. I could barely make it around the block at first, but I forced myself to try new exercises and even joined a gym. This is when things really started to change. I forced my swollen, oversized feet into the bike pedals in a spin class, not caring about the judgmental stares from the group. I was there for me and no one else. Since my buddies also belonged to the gym, I soon started to follow their weight-lifting routines, modified to my capabilities at the time. And so I ran, spun till I cried, lifted weight after weight, until the pounds started to melt away. I knew then that I was a winner, and that I was NOT losing this bet.

Success in a silver moon suit

That particular New Year's Day, the day of the wager, I shall never forget. By now, many were following my journey, so a large crowd gathered to see my final weigh-in results. Exhausted from running all night in a silver moon suit (such as the one in the movie *Vision Quest*) designed to draw water from the body, I dragged myself to the gym and up onto the scale. As you may anticipate, I did indeed reach my goal.

I won, and I never felt better in my life!

In summary, the core of my success was—and still is—based upon the following:

1. I got clean and sober. I was mentored by friend and artist Peter Tunney, and I am very grateful.
2. I changed my attitude from "I want" to "I will."
3. I set small goals, rather than being over-whelmed with the end goal. For instance, "I'll lose three to five pounds this week," not "I need to lose 200 pounds."
4. I started with small changes and made gradual adjustments along the way.
5. I incorporated high-fiber meals and snacks to keep me full with fewer calories.
6. I began exercising at my own pace. A walk around the block or five minutes on the tread-mill was my start. I increased as my endurance increased.
7. I dropped the processed dead foods, and added living raw foods. "Goodbye comfort foods, I no longer need you!"
8. I juiced fruits and vegetables daily.
9. I used tools such as organic dark chocolate to satisfy cravings and to fill me up before meals or after.

10. I researched! The Internet has amazing resources, such as weight-loss tools, inspirational writings, calorie counters, and more.
11. I prayed and gave thanks for all I have and all I was to achieve.
12. I believed in myself, in my body's innate ability to heal, and in the life I deserved.

To all seeking change: Take action
My story of triumphant success quickly spread locally and nationally, inspiring fellow health-seekers to reach their goals. Another seemingly impossible dream became reality for me when I was featured as a guest on the Emmy-award-winning show, *The Doctors* and then on *Oprah*. Can you believe that? And the once-in-a-lifetime opportunities did not stop there! Obesity and addictions are both perilous, leading to tragedy for a great many Americans and countless others worldwide. As a token of gratitude for sharing with millions the story of how I overcame both of them, world renowned plastic surgeon Dr. Jason Pozner gifted me with a complimentary extended abdominoplasty (tummy-tuck) to remove excess skin, common after such a massive weight loss.

My life had been completely transformed, and now I was so blessed to have the help of professionals to finish the job.

Motivated by a steadfast desire to share my story with those who may be affected by obesity or addiction, I meticulously documented the pain, struggles, failures, successes, and even humor of my journey in hope that one day my experience would bring inspiration to many. It was then that my first publication, the book *Mind Over Body,* was conceived.

Mind Over Body is a collection of stories chronicling my fall from grace and rise back from the near-dead. The book depicts my fight from the depths of hell. In order to reach my distant, colossal goals, I did it "climbing one inch at a time," a quote from the speech given by Al Pacino in the movie *Any Given Sunday.* My entire journey is documented in the book, including links to self-help information, recipes, and my mentors, ready and waiting to help you, too.

Finally, to all who are contemplating change, I urge you to take action. As Peter Tunney is fond of saying, "The time is always now!"

About the Author

Peter Ajello, originally from Saddle River, New Jersey, is an author, Life Coach and motivational speaker who comes from a family of artisan candle-makers. The youngest of four brothers, he attended Pope John Paul II High School in Boca Raton, Florida, where he excelled athletically, playing varsity football for four years. Peter went on to attend Johnson and Wales University in Providence, Rhode Island. Currently, he resides in Fort Lauderdale, Florida and is the owner and National Sales Manager of Satin Finish Concrete Polishing and Floor Restoration. Peter has also written *Pete's Chocolate Diet Book*, along with a motivational rock album on the way and a screenplay in the works, which will bring *Mind Over Body* to cinematic life.

Peter's amazing story has been featured on *Dr. Oz*, *Live Healthy with Adam Kuperstein*, NBC, AOL, Fox News, *The Today Show* in Australia, on Fuji TV in Japan, and in more than over 5,000 print articles across the world. He reached millions of viewers as a special guest of Bret Michaels on an episode of the OWN Network hit series, *Oprah's Lifeclass*.

To reach Peter, to purchase Pete's Organic Weight-loss Chocolates or copies of *Mind Over Body*, go to PeterAjello.com. You can also follow Peter on Facebook and YouTube for healthy tips and daily motivation.

The Real Skinny On My Anorexia

Erin Garcia

As I got ready to appear in a recent video shoot for my fancy new coaching website, I noticed that I had picked out a hot pink blouse that showed off my stomach's newly acquired "jelly roll." Yes, I am now moderately overweight, which is a new phenomenon. At first I didn't know whether to laugh in response or to be disgusted, but in that moment I saw the awesome poetic justice in it, and perhaps even the Divine sense of humor, all "rolled" into one (pun intended).

The irony was that, just as I was about to tell the story of my eating disorder on camera, I realized I could now literally show definite proof of my "over-recovery" as well!

I am an energetic sixty-year-old wife, mother, and grandmother. My husband, Steve, and I have been married now for thirty-nine years and ten days, as of this writing. We have five amazing grown children who have blessed us with twelve grandchildren. I would love a "baker's dozen," so now all we need is one of my children deciding to make the leap and add to their families.

I recently had the entire family over for my husband's birthday, and quipped that we now need to find a bigger house with an upstairs game room to accommodate our grandchildren, eleven of whom are under eleven years old, six of them mischievous grand*sons*! My son-in-law retorted, "In a bigger house you would miss the direct impact of all this chaos." He has a point.

Friends visiting our home during a family gathering, as they are inclined to do, often remark on how much fun we have, and how much joy is in evidence. We have our moments and our disagreements, as any family does, but there's something undeniably special going on when the twenty or so of us get together, something truly inspirational.

That unspoken element always present is the fact that my husband and I truly *cherish* each and every one of the precious lives we've been gifted with. Each and every one of my family feels truly valued. Steve and I intentionally convey this message to each, and we do it often.

I shouldn't even be here to tell this story

You see, I am the survivor of a potentially deadly eating disorder called anorexia nervosa, which I have suffered from since around the age of ten, continuing into my twenties.

I met my husband when I was twenty years old and working on one of my many ten-pound-weight-loss-plunges. At the heart of my story is how Steve showed up in the nick of time to save my life. I was ninety-three pounds at five- foot-six. (I'm of medium build, and I won't tell you my size now, but let's just say I was almost half the woman I am now, ha!).

When I first met my husband, I could barely eat at all. My hair was thinning, my skin was overly dry, and I would often have blackouts. I no longer had normal monthly cycles, and I was weak and withdrawn. I was electrolyte-challenged, which affected my energy tremendously, even though being anything but energetic was normally very unlike me. If Steve made a meal, he knew he would end up eating most of my portion. He knew something was wrong, but couldn't put his finger on it.

But wait, let me back up a bit...
I am from the sixties and seventies era, when no one really knew anything about eating disorders. As a matter of fact, until the tragedy of Karen Carpenter's death during her attempt to recover from anorexia, no one really knew how dangerous eating disorders are, and how widespread. As a 2005 *Newsweek* magazine article revealed, "Research shows that anorexia, which affects 2.5 million Americans, has the highest mortality rate of *any* mental illness...About half of anorexics recover." (Some other more recent studies have said that only one-third recover.)

The article continues, "Anorexia (which literally means 'loss of appetite') is a mental illness defined by an obsession with food and acute anxiety over gaining weight, affecting...teens and young women on the verge of growing up..." (*Newsweek*, December 5, 2005).

The situation has worsened considerably since that article was written. There are Facebook groups dedicated to the eating disordered who are seeking recovery, and what stories they share! My own dysfunctional family system and chaotic home environment would prove to be a classic seedbed for my battle with an eating disorder.

We were a middle-income suburban family who

seemed normal enough. However, inside our four walls was a home ridden with conflict, denial, and detachment, creating no safety zone to express emotions or personal needs. An anorexic in families such as these becomes like a sponge, absorbing the unspoken and unexpressed turbulence around them. I'm sure I picked up on both of my parents' *and* my older sister's "stuff"… in fact, I became an expert at absorbing the fallout from a range of unexpressed emotions, unspoken disapproval, a variety of false attitudes, and detachment. I took these on as my own burden—a silent cry uttered in an effort to bring order to chaos, a cry my traumatized parents could not hear.

My mom had suffered from severe manic depression, now called bipolar disorder, since her teens. Back then, they used shock treatment a lot for this disorder, and I'm not so sure that didn't have a worse effect on her than the disorder itself. She would go in and out of institutions, and when she was home she would retreat to her bed for two weeks at a time in her depressive cycles, only to come out like a whirlwind and—oops, there she is, alarming us by her next round of manic activities. We never knew what we would be put through at any given time. We were only children, for heaven's sake!

A parent to my own parent
I always felt responsible to somehow parent my own mother, as if such a thing were possible. My sister,

being the elder by three years, would cope in her own way, coming up with creative ways to manage her own emotions and thereby containing her reactions to our mother's manic episodes. I must say, we both stayed very busy with every possible activity, class, and club known to the modern world. My sister is a gifted artist, pianist, tennis player... the list goes on and on. We became very good at accomplishing things!

My dad was Mom's third husband. He had been in both World War II and the Korean War, and wanted to go career in the military, while mom did not agree. Though they had a "Scarlett O'Hara/Rhett Butler" type of intensity to their relationship, largely due to her histrionics, my father was bent on keeping our family's outward appearance looking "normal" at all costs. He couldn't even begin to know the price we would all pay for this decision.

Dad soon became a "former-military-man-turned-executive," with a highly perfectionistic profile. Managing the ongoing drama surrounding my mom's episodes was definitely like trying to control a hurricane for him, so he resorted to taking it out on my sister and me, making demands with impossibly high standards for both our accomplishment levels and our personal conduct. He was a deeply private man and people respected him greatly, but all I got to see was the "home" version of my father—affectionate one moment and horribly raging the next. This is the perfect breeding ground for a people-pleaser, and it turned me into one, for sure.

Hungry at the heart level

I had my secret ways of coping. Actually, maybe they weren't so secret. At family gatherings, during all of this, I would hear comments being made about me, such as "She doesn't eat enough to keep a bird alive," and similar remarks. I was constantly asked why I wasn't finishing my dinner. I recall secretly throwing a lot of my food away and feeling a pervasive, unexplained shame, especially at meal times. I had always experienced stomach pain before, during, and after a meal. An omnipresent, undefined pressure always seemed to loom about me, along with feelings of having to be *more*, do *more*, and always—above all—to do everything absolutely right! This thought process demanded that I constantly deprive myself of the joy of just *being in the moment*.

Mere "being" would never be enough.

My inner dialogue began to say to me throughout the day, "*Erin, no. Stifle it. You can't be hungry. You do not have permission to have hunger, or to be satisfied. You don't have the right. You don't deserve to eat, or to live life with joy. You don't deserve to... live!*"

Lurking behind the fog of this reality was a true self-hatred, in spite of my very outgoing, bubbly personality. And it's never really gone: To this day I have to consciously cast this lie down. Certain events and personality types can trigger it, but the important thing is that now I know, in the deepest part of my true self, that it's a lie from the very pit of hell.

I know that denying my body of the most basic human function—eating—speaks of a deeply troubled heart. I was truly "hungry" at a heart level, starved for normal love and appropriate attention.

My extreme distress led to an even deeper, even more damaging form of denial—I no longer felt I had the right to *any* need at all. Such is the vicious cycle of self-hatred. As Peggy Claude-Pierre puts it, "I have heard many people describe eating disorders as a consequence of low esteem... I believe the problem goes far deeper. In fact, I find they have no sense of self or identity, except for the fulfillment of their extremely subjective perception of others' expectations."

The hole that self-love should fill

The worst of my eating disorder was intensified by a typical drive to overachieve. I was intensely performance-oriented, with the usual distorted body imaging that is classically associated with eating disorders. I kept busy on a manic scale, involved with several sports and the pom squad, while maintaining an AP level of academics. As if that were not enough, I took on lead roles in our high school musicals. All of this fueled my obsession with looking good.

I was plagued by my false identity. During this most crucial of developmental phases, adolescence, I was enslaved by a heart-level belief system consisting of a network of lies, self-condemnation, deep-seated shame, and guilt. It's as though a tyrannical inner critic took over inside me, raging at me with nonstop negative self-talk.

I would hear: *"You're a fat slob," "You're no good*

because you're not thin enough," "*You'll never be good enough for God or anybody else.*" I began to echo the lethal self-talk a client recently suffered through, convincing herself that "*I would rather be dead than fat!*"

It is clear, as I indicated earlier, that my anorexia was an attempt on my part to fill a deep hole inside of me that I had created from a severe lack of self-love. Cynthia French, author of *Humanville*, says, "I know that every story of recovery is unique, but there are similarities that intertwine all of our experiences. I believe that we are born with the birthright to love ourselves. God gives us that blessing because His love is so unconditional and pure. However, we are influenced by those around us and our environment from day one, so it's understandable that we could learn to despise ourselves if we let vicious, unkind, and demeaning words affect the way we think of ourselves."

Dr. Gregory Jantz describes well the spiritual nature of the anorexic's inner struggle:

"Self-hate argues against the truth of God's love for you and the great value you have. The negative inner messages of self-hate deafen your ability to hear God's voice singing over you as a precious, valued human being."

Somehow, in the midst of my deepest pain, I began to hear—faintly at first—the sweet sound of my heavenly Father's song over me, and was able to begin the long process of seeing myself as God sees me, and with it the equally long journey of recovery.

My earthly father died of cancer when I was eighteen,

and my mother took her own life when I was twenty. I lost both sets of grandparents within three to four years, but my Father God had powerfully revealed to me that "He would never leave me or forsake me."

I would go on to meet and marry Steve Garcia, a wonderful sensitive Christian man who loves to COOK (God's sense of humor once again), and who was sent in the nick of time to literally save my life, there is no doubt in my mind about that. I recovered and gave birth to my lively five, as I said, and they have produced our tremendous twelve. We all sing to God's Glory, celebrating each other and life fully.

Not a day goes by that I don't hear my Father singing over me with great pleasure, loud and clear.

And I am fed.

About the Author

Erin Garcia is a Pastoral Counselor at Plumbline Ministries in Tulsa, OK. She is a Professional Certified Coach with her own practice, Real Skinny Life Coaching. Erin is finishing her book, *The Real Skinny on My Anorexia*, which will be published in 2015. Contact her at Erin@RealSkinnyLifeCoaching.com or check out her website, RealSkinnyLifeCoaching.com, "For Those Hungry For More!"

Hooked on Healers

Susan Jacobs

For decades I have depended on alternative healers to help me get through, physically, mentally, and spiritually. And I've had the best. My yoga practice, my work as a marketing consultant, and love of travel have taken me around the world, allowing me to meet an abundance of natural and holistic healers from New York to Ghana, Haiti to California, Ecuador to Paris, London to Viet Nam, and various stops along the way. Many of them have literally and figuratively helped save my life.

I've worn acupuncture needles over every inch of my body; been burned with moxibustion; spat on in an African libation ceremony by elder tribesmen; diagnosed via pendulums, pulse, tongue, eyes, and abdomen; taken full-moon baths in flower petals; stared at a colored light through a telescope-type gadget; been steamed with herbs in an I-Love-Lucy-type box with just my head sticking out; drank special teas that included ingredients better for me not to know, that took hours to cook and days to expel the smell from my apartment; put off making decisions until consulting my astrologer and tarot card reader; drank customized concoctions of Bach flower remedies and potions; beat pillows while screaming and crying, followed by visualizing positive healing energy coming into my heart; and had an excruciating massage from an elder voodoo practitioner.

That's a small sampling of my healing specialties, while my regular, day-to-day supply of practitioners included a chiropractor, atlas orthoganist, naturopath, homeopath, acupuncturist, nutritionist, shaman, herbologist, astrologer, tarot-card reader, holistic eye doctor, and shiatsu and massage therapists.

And, lest I needed help in the middle of the night, I was fully equipped with a library of self-help books covering the New Age, Buddhism, as well as such basic spiritually uplifting resources as Louise Hay, Marianne Williamson, Deepak Chopra, Eckhart Tolle, Collin Tipping, Bernie Siegel, Caroline Myss, Mother Teresa, Pema Chodron, John-Roger, Julia Cameron, Jack Kornfield, Neale Donald Walsch, Esther Hicks, James Redfield, Thich Nhat Hanh, the Dalai Lama, Steven Pressfield, Yogi Bhajan, and a variety of Al-Anon daily readings.

Just to make sure I continue to stay on track, I still subscribe to inspirational emails from Daily Guru, Daily Kabbalah, I Believe God Wants You to Know, I Am A Woman (Yogi Bhajan), Positively Positive, The Pleasure Team, Cynthia Occelli, Christine Arylo, and a daily horoscope.

There's only one problem with all this, and it took hitting rock bottom for me to see it.

I was no longer free to enjoy these gifts. *I was hooked on healers.*

Earth Shoes and elevated energies
My connection to alternative, natural healing, and self-help began when I was a teenager. As the daughter of the founders of the original Earth Shoe company, I spent ages ten to seventeen, which was during the 70s, surrounded by hippies who worked in the commune-like store downstairs from our apartment on 17th Street in New York City.

Anne Kalsø, the inventor of these unique shoes, was a 60-ish-year-old Danish yoga teacher who tested her new styles by walking 500 miles in the Faroe Islands. Despite their cult status, the shoes were actually unsightly, with an exaggerated "negative heel," lower than the toe, which replicates walking barefoot in sand. Anne, a perfect product of her time, agreed to meet my parents, Eleanor and Raymond Jacobs, only after requesting their birth dates and having their astrological charts done. She also made sure they had never been in the shoe business. As my father's obituary in the *New York Times* put it, twenty years ago, my parents "were astrologically correct," so Anne granted them the rights to distribute her shoes in the US.

I mention this because, between Anne and the employees, I was exposed at a young age to an alternative lifestyle that neither my family nor our friends knew anything about. We were rapidly introduced to yoga, meditation, shiatsu, Reiki, the power of positive thinking, *Be Here Now*, Krishnamurti, auras, astrology, vegetarian and macrobiotic diets, and much more. Every day my sister, Laura, and I would run home from the United Nations International School to hang out in the store, flirting with the male employees, doing homework, and helping customers, while the staff regaled us with stories about life, love, sex, and non-traditional lifestyles. I was precocious, and had a PhD in flirting at a young age, so was fully in my element. Laura, two years younger than I and more straight-laced, still developed intense crushes on the cute guys, and we both often fell innocently but insanely in love.

Melting, mantras, macrobiotics

It was through our close connection with Earth Shoes that I learned about Japanese shiatsu acupressure, my first foray into holistic healing. I had my first session at fifteen with Ohashi, who had arrived in New York from Japan. I melted under his touch. Although the sessions were painful, when it was over energy surged through my body, and I felt amazing. I booked appointments with him on a regular basis, primarily as a preventive measure, to keep my chi (energy) flowing properly and my organs and glands in balance. Who knew, when I was trekking to his innocuous West 55th Street office, that he would go on to become a preeminent force in spreading shiatsu across the US?

My family was introduced to macrobiotic cooking by the Earth Shoe employees, who brought in a macrobiotic chef to prepare us a gourmet meal once a week for twelve weeks—although I am still not sure *gourmet* and *macrobiotic* belong in the same sentence! The chef was as dedicated to her cooking as she was to her other occupation: raising twelve kids, one born in each zodiac sign. (Ah, the seventies!) We listened, we learned, but after the first week we'd sneak out to Zookie's Deli on Third Avenue for a hotdog before dinner so we didn't have to eat as much of our special meal.

During this period, my mother was enamored

with the Beatles and their connection with the Maharishi and Transcendental Meditation. She convinced the rest of our family to become equally impressed, which we did. This included a strange ritual involving filling a white handkerchief with white rice and spreading the rice throughout a park. Once we all did that and received our secret mantras, we became the family that meditated together. My parents instituted a policy for the Earth Shoe staff—free TM training after three months of employment. Suddenly it was a family and company experience! We would meditate with the employees in the basement on seats from the back of a van. Sworn to the famous TM rule never to disclose your mantra, only years later, when Laura and I played True Confessions, did we discover we were given the same mantra.

I practiced TM for a number of years, meditating like clockwork twice a day. It may actually have taken a slight edge off my teenage delinquency (I can't imagine the havoc I would have caused without TM!), but my mother may disagree.

My family was way ahead of my peer group when it came to the holistic life experience. Through my teenage years and into my early twenties, meditation, Tai Chi, yoga, and shiatsu were staples in my life. That's also when I began reading spiritual books and learning about Buddhism. I remain a perpetual wanna-be-Buddhist. It was at this time when I came to believe that we create our own reality, illnesses/conditions, and also have the power to self-heal.

The man who literally turned my head

My first real understanding of the power of the mind-body connection was when I was nineteen. I had been taking a dress off over my head when my head literally got stuck facing my right shoulder. I was going through a stressful time and holding everything in my neck and shoulders. The muscle spasms pulled my vertebrae out of alignment. In a desperate state, I found my first chiropractor. Dr. R. spent a week taking care of me: nurturing me, helping me heal, and offering a shoulder to cry on. Within a week, he had my head facing straight and me back to normal. Well, normal except I was convinced I was in love with this godlike man who literally turned my head!

Since thinking before taking action wasn't my specialty, I wrote Dr. R. a long love letter, pretty much offering him anything my mind, body, and spirit could give. This was before computers, so I wrote, stamped, and mailed the letter. Once the mail slot closed, I panicked, "Oh crap, what have I done?" But it was too late.

The call came a few days later. I was certain it was going to be his reciprocal expression of love, but alas, it was not. Flattered, he defined his doctor/patient boundary, which he wouldn't cross, at least not with this starry-eyed, innocent nineteen-year-old! Embarrassed doesn't begin to describe how I felt, so I offered to go to another chiropractor. He said there was no need and I remained his patient for years. We found a good balance, friendly flirting but nothing more.

My next significant healer was my first acupuncturist, whom I also fell in love with. This ended up as a serious relationship that became the perfect incubator for my growing dependency on healers and spiritual teachers. If I felt the slightest twinge, mentally, physically, or spiritually, I went running for a treatment, for words of wisdom, and advice (despite his being ten years younger than I). We meditated together, cooked brown rice in every form possible, and inevitably I got yelled at for living from ego and not spirit. I never made a move without his direction and approval. I was in my own mini-cult, a disciple serving my guru.

A heroin-level habit

This was a dependency as powerful as I imagine substance addiction to be. And I took that dependency into my subsequent relationships, each manifesting some variation on the same theme.

I finally hit rock bottom at the end of an emotionally abusive relationship, after which I found my way to Al-Anon twelve-step meetings. It was there where I finally realized that, not only had I been dependent on men most of my life, but also on healers, on seeking advice, guidance, direction, and wanting to be told what do by anyone who would indulge me. This was tough to realize, and I rejected it at first.

While Al-Anon helped get me through one of the most challenging periods of my life, it also freed me to see that I do have the answers within. I resisted, but slowly learned that I can trust my intuition and the guidance of my Higher Power. I found that if I meditate, I can conquer what is known in the East as monkey mind—the CNN news crawl of thoughts running through my head. Doing yoga or a moving form of meditation with repetitive motion connected to breath (such as running), also quiets my mind, and the answers become clear. When in doubt, a good piece of dark chocolate also helps!

I loved going to Al-Anon meetings, where I had a different audience every day as I received attention, sympathy, and support.

My next revelation: I was dependent on Al-Alon meetings.

I had become Queen Victim, loving that role and all that came with it, until someone said, "Victims aren't sexy."

It was like Cher's famous "Snap out of it" slap that she gives Nicholas Cage in *Moonstruck* after he says he loves her. *Slap.* That was all I needed to hear. I was now a middle-aged single woman, and *unsexy* was the last way I wanted to be described.

Answering to the master gland

Over the past twenty years, there's been a major sub-plot in my life that has tested all my good intentions, as I've been dealing with a hyperthyroid and Graves disease. At its worst, my resting heartbeat was over 100 BPM, which could have been extremely danger-ous. Conventional doctors wanted me to follow the standard treatment of drinking radioactive iodine to kill my thyroid, causing me to ultimately become hypothyroid, and on medicine for the rest of my life.

If I chose that treatment, I would have been so radioactive afterwards that I wouldn't have been able to be around children or animals for a couple of days. Sure, sign me up, that's right up my alley.

So there I was, face-to-face with a harsh reality. Could I live by my belief system to its ultimate conclusion: that I created this condition as a means to look at what was going on with my life, and ultimately heal myself? Sounded great on paper, but I was about to make life-saving or life-threatening decisions, and suddenly it was confusing and terrifying. Should I take the dangerous, though seemingly "safe" Western medical route, covered by insurance, or trust my now expansive network of healers, none of whom were covered by insurance?

I chose the latter, a decision accompanied by my having to endure the forceful opinions of my family, friends, and endocrinologist, who fired me as his patient because I wouldn't succumb to radical Western treatments.

My healing was a long, hard journey that was accomplished 95% holistically, the exceptions being two eye surgeries for the Graves disease, a year on the thyroid drug PTU before my body rejected it with a negative liver reaction, and a short stint on beta-blockers to protect my heart.

Throughout the twenty-year process, I depended on my primary holistic team of trusted advisors and practitioners in New York, Ghana, and California. I still had so many layers of self doubt that once again I began running to others for answers, direction, guidance, nurturing, and the TLC I couldn't give myself. At the same time I was opening to a whole new level of self-awareness, as I read Caroline Myss's *Anatomy of the Spirit* and Pema Chodron's *When Things Fall Apart*.

The deeper challenge: remaining conscious

It was then that a deeper level of healing began.

From these books, I became a much more active and conscious participant in my healing, not solely expecting that a treatment method would do the trick. This perspective requires tremendous energy, focus, and discipline to maintain, and even though I'm aware of the benefits and have seen the proven results, sustaining this level of conscious living remains a constant challenge.

Diet and lifestyle played a big part in my healing, but I believe the most important factor was my becoming able to *see* (Graves disease affects the eyes) that I needed to *speak* (thyroid is part of the throat) and live my truth. When I started doing that, my blood numbers and symptoms balanced out.

Now I can report that for the past three years my thyroid has been balanced, and so is my life. I sit here reflecting on all that's been, the choices and mistakes I've made, and lessons learned. I'm healthy, strong, and generally at peace. When stress starts to mount, I rely on everything that I've learned, and when still in doubt, I call my mother!!!

I use healers on an as-needed basis for a tune-up, although I still get a tarot card reading every three months and follow my monthly horoscope. These keep me feeling connected to something bigger than myself, a universal community where there's an explanation for why, when, and how things are happening.

It took me decades of chasing healers, gurus, and wanna-be gurus, of tasting their Kool-Aid, countless years of hoping to be enlightened before I realized that I am my BFF (best friend forever) and my best, most trusted guru. When I'm disciplined, with a daily practice of three simple actions—Kundalini Yoga, journaling, and meditation—life flows, stress is minimized, and I receive answers and a sense of direction.

It is with true gratitude that I thank all those along the way who helped me navigate my own road map, the one that brought me back home. And frankly, it's a comfort to know that whenever I get lazy and start to lose my way, I still have my most trusted healers on speed-dial!

About the Author

Susan Jacobs, who has holistically healed a hyperthyroid condition and Graves Disease, has travelled the world, working on projects in Africa, Haiti,

Europe, and the US. The daughter of Raymond and Eleanor Jacobs, the founders of the original Earth Shoe company in America, she has been involved with holistic living and alternative medicine since she was ten, learning to navigate and integrate Western and Eastern medicine for her own healing. One of her challenges has been maintaining a spiritual life while working in the entertainment industry for the past twenty-five years as a marketing, communications, and branding strategist, event producer, and project manager. A freelance writer living in Brooklyn, her articles have appeared in *Aquarian Times*, *Spirituality & Health*, *PR Week*, and *IndieWire*. Her newest venture, BlueZan Consulting, creates marketing, branding, and communications strategies, campaigns, and events, focusing primarily on socially responsible, cause-driven projects. Her expertise is enriched by her life-changing experiences in different cultures while traveling off the beaten path. Susan is currently writing a book about her thyroid journey for the Round House Press.

Exercise, My Refuge, My Nightmare

Betsy Jennings

Looking back, I seem to have always been riddled with fear, rejection, and pain.

I longed for control over these feelings, and it came in the form of movement, starvation, bingeing, and purging.

As a young girl, I was totally captivated with moving and expressing myself, especially to music. I would feel alive and full of purpose and peace whenever I focused on the talent I was blessed with—my ability to move effortlessly, to tap dance or pirouette with my spirit.

But then I began to change my focus, away from my dream of becoming a dancer with a possible future on stage, and toward a future of fear and confusion. My beloved movement, my practice, had morphed from a place of refuge and protection into an activity of insanity and punishment.

As I began to gain weight, my desire to move my body escalated even further into an obsession with unstoppable movement that took on a life of its own. Now I felt I couldn't control myself or regulate the changes I was going through. Excessive exercise, self-starvation, and rituals around food became my daily departure from feelings that I could no longer tolerate or understand. Though my body was changing the way nature intended it to, I had no idea what was going on externally and—oh my gosh—internally.

You see, while I was growing and changing into a young woman, there were many messages of shame coming from the people around me, including my peers and family members who were preoccupied with appearance and weight. I was often picked on for my appearance and the way my body was built. I did not know how to handle this, so I concluded that since it felt like everyone was against me, why not be against myself as well?

Coming from a family background of addiction, I naturally sought whatever would numb the way I felt about myself. So, from age twelve on, alcohol, drugs, and the need for approval became my new obsessions.

I felt extremely uncomfortable with my changing body, especially around the beginning of tenth grade. That was also when I had a major bout with mononucleosis that landed me in bed for many months, while I filled up my time poring over books on weight loss and dieting.

Obsessing behind closed doors

I locked myself behind closed doors during this time, supposedly "resting," while I was secretly performing countless situps and leg lifts, trying to banish my anxieties and confusion about my body, my place in the world, and my place in my family.

This was the year that the excessive preoccupation with keeping food journals and establishing rigid eating patterns began to strangle the choices I made, or should I say, *could not make* in my life.

High school was both one big party and a source of ongoing angst for me. Because I was really in the pits of addiction at that time, my shame, anger, and self-loathing grew. Self-medication was the only way for me to get through. To make things worse, all the weight that I lost through excessive exercise and starvation crept back on.

After high school I reluctantly went to college, where I spent most of my time drinking and actively bingeing and purging. I failed miserably my first semester and never went back.

I then moved to Alaska, thinking life would be better, but it was more of the same. It was during this painful time, when I was feeling absolutely out of control, that I lost my mother, who had been diagnosed in 1982 with pancreatic cancer and died soon after. The two years following her death were horrendous. In 1984 I finally surrendered and entered rehab.

I had lost my precious ability to move with ease and grace.

The familiar obsessions began again, at a much higher intensity, however, after I detoxed in that rehab. It was a rude awakening when I realized I was at a higher weight then ever, and heavily bloated. Drinking, non-existent health care, and late-night food binges to fill the void and to quiet the screaming of shame, loneliness, and fear all took a tremendous toll on my body.

So, sober in one respect only, I replaced alcohol with excessive starvation, bingeing/purging, and compulsive exercise. Day one of this latest phase actually started in rehab, when I took any opportunity to endlessly walk, and walk some more.

As if this were not enough, I started playing

around with food till my insides were in shambles. *What have I done to myself?* I silently cried out. *How could I have let myself go down so deeply?* I felt new fears coming alive, so I needed to walk even more in order to pound them down. If I could no longer numb myself with substances, what would I become? How would I be able to live within this body that I grew to hate so much?

Drinking Karen Carpenter's killer

So my days in early recovery were spent in endless walking. I told everyone that I was trying to get in shape, but what I was doing was hiding from the fear of living life without alcohol and the anxiety of not knowing who I was. Every step I took was on my quest to banish fear. With every step I pounded out shame, fear, and self-hatred.

A year later, in 1985, I entered inpatient treatment at an eating disorder clinic.

I truly do not remember exactly why I decided to go into treatment for my eating disorder at that particular time. Clearly fear and even desperation, those effective motivators, were present. I can't say that I got better in terms of my behaviors right away, either. When I was discharged, my combined bulimia/exercise addictions actually intensified, and fear and unresolved grief started to make their appearance in my soul. It was too much for me to handle, so I continued to pound the pain and eat away the self-loathing.

Then I had a couple of episodes with ipecac syrup, using it to induce vomiting. This is the stuff that killed Karen Carpenter. It brought me to my knees in surrender. Only then did I stop the bulimia. And I mean it came to a complete halt.

Perhaps enough of me came back to life through my sobriety to allow that surrender to happen. Perhaps I realized that God had equipped me with enough skills to handle life on life's terms, after all, and I no longer needed to gorge on food and exercise.

And I will not overlook the fact that my body was simply not holding me up any more.

One good thing about my time at the clinic was that I had access to a valuable aspect of treatment while I was there, a process that brought in family members. You see, most addictions have their roots in family issues—at least for me that was the case. I come from generations of substance abuse and inadequate coping skills. I have heard it said that people like me are the healthy ones in such a family system, since while we are acting out we are at least telling the world we are in pain, that something is wrong. We are communicating.

Have trampoline, will travel
But it wasn't over. Even my façade of "normal life," as I began to teach fitness classes at a local YMCA, was designed to keep my secrets hidden. Wholesome, right? No, this turned out to be four hours of punishment in the morning and four hours of the

same again in the late afternoon. I was a prisoner to the appearance of being in shape and leading others to the same goal. I was still in bondage, while convincing myself that what I was doing was a form of protection.

I began to suffer physically. My knees were in constant pain, but I would find a way to keep going. My legs would tremble and give out. The nerves in my feet were shot. But I would always find a way to keep going.

Unable to stop, I even traveled with a mini trampoline. When I visited family, the trampoline would go with me. I had to know that I had my safe place to escape to, and exercise was it. Situations such as family gatherings created anxiety for me. I feared that I didn't look thin enough. I feared that I wasn't good enough. Only exercise, my refuge, allowed me to feel that I was okay.

Finally, my body totally gave out. My knees could not hold me up any longer. I landed in the operating room for surgery on both knees. Eventually I also had surgery for nerve damage in my foot. Because I had so much pain up and down my legs, I was diagnosed with Chronic Pain Syndrome, but tests revealed nothing.

Unbelievably, I found another crutch in my attempt to make life bearable... *actual crutches*. They had been given to me by doctors to help me get around, but instead I used them as a way to continue the insanity of excessive exercise.

Crutches!

I was living a life totally devoted to purging an imaginary internal poison.

My quest for perfection, along with a necessary detachment from myself, were destroying me, physically and spiritually. Something had to give. My life centered around my time at the gym or on the treadmill. Relationships took second place, until I could reach the endorphin high that exercise gave me. Then, and only then, could I present myself to another person and to the world.

The origin of my escape from all this is about as mysterious as what led me into the obsession.

As I slowly started to really live life, I became able to face the reality that I had to be honest with myself. It dawned on me that it was time to look at the residue inside of me before I could let go of the excessive rituals around exercise that had run my life.

Living under the white flag of freedom
Somewhere in those dark days, I began to surrender. I raised a white flag and began to embrace the fact that I mattered, that I was not junk, and that I could learn to genuinely nurture and care for my body.

I found that I could actually trust myself, and that letting go had the power to open up a whole new appreciation of myself and the life I had in front of me.

All I knew was that I was beginning to live sanely for the first time. I managed not only to go to college, but to graduate with high honors, earning a four-year degree. I quickly found a job that I absolutely loved that involved helping people. I began to see that there was more to life than hiding behind leg lifts and stomach crunches.

I am still not perfect, by any means. But I follow healthy instincts now. I start my day off with prayer, meditation, and then an hour of treadmill time, then weights. I do experience anxiety if I am not able to start my day with my routine. You see, I am *in recovery*, not recovered. My old way of life left residual effects in my belief system that I fight against, ever so gently.

Some days the residue is a bit persistent than others, and those are the days when I must practice heavy doses of affirmations, prayer, laughter, and just plain thankfulness to be alive and free. Maturity has helped a great deal. Children and a supportive husband are a bonus, as well.

Having a career that I love, one where I can help others, allows me to see how selfish I was when I permitted myself to be held in bondage to addictive behaviors and thought patterns.

I still struggle, though to a lesser degree, with the temptation to play around with eating too much, followed by calculating how much exercise I then need. But exercise just does not have the mental stronghold on me that it used to have.

I rely on exercise now more as a mood booster. I definitely feel better after exercising. Don't get me wrong, though—I do get anxious if I can't get one good walk in, or more, if time allows. I do still have somewhat of a dependence on exercise. I am wired for some form of movement. Just the other week, I was preparing for a talk on grief and recovery, searching my heart for memories of my own grief and for family events where I am sure grief has never been acknowledged, let alone resolved. As I pondered, I found myself pounding the pain I was feeling.

It showed in the painfully familiar way I was walking. There it was again, clear as a bell: the connection between my grief and the pounding of my footsteps in a vain attempt to connect with spirit.

I am a work in progress.

Happiness at being me is starting to trickle in more and more. To be honest, though, there are days when I would love to start a new fitness program, so I can look like the woman Hollywood says I should look like.

Today, however, I know myself enough to know that I am highly susceptible to such deceiving messages from the culture we live in. I replace those cravings with a strong sense that I am beautiful, strong, and courageous *just as I am*. I would rather hold on to that belief than what the culture around me says I should be.

As I learn to embrace myself, I find I can hug my flaws and work with what God has given me. I believe today that I am not the damaged goods that I have thought I was for so many years. I am liking the company of family and friends more than the isolation of a lonely walk or another set of leg lifts.

Today I can dance in a spirit of joy and gratitude once again. I can walk when I want to and can stop and smell the flowers if I wish. I am more at ease with myself as I become more skillful at being present to the life I am so thankful to have.

Today I walk if I choose and run if I'd rather. Pounding out the pain is no longer an option for me. Living life to the fullest, loving with every ounce of energy that I have, and taking risks with my heart by connecting with others and God far outweigh any mile I have walked, lap I have swum, or calorie I have counted. There is no winning that way.

Occasionally, I may lose focus or wish for something different, but the difference is that today I don't stay there long. My spirit dances and my soul is free. I am once more captivated by just being me.

I am told that I am beautifully and wonderfully made.

I believe that now.

About the Author

Betsy Jennings, CVACC, CLBC, has a ferocious passion for mentoring, teaching, and motivating. With over twenty-five years in the social services/case management/addiction fields and almost thirty years in personal recovery, she was called to train and become certified in coaching and mentoring women at any point in their journeys of addiction and recovery. Having found purpose in her journey with her own addictions, she instills hope into the lives of others. Betsy lives in Endicott, New York with her husband, Ron, and their three boys. Contact Betsy through her website, HopeAndBreakthroughCoaching.com.

Manning Up:
The Poem on the
Stationhouse Wall

Jeremy Manning

It's Monday morning in San Francisco, 2005 as I wake up from a three-day crystal meth bender. My boyfriend is already up and ready for work. I'm baffled by his ability to pull himself together. He's reaching for his keys and I'm reaching for my phone to call in sick. My hands are so weak and shaky that I can barely manage to dial the number where I can leave a voicemail for my boss. I've done this so many times that I don't even make up excuses anymore. I just say, "It's Jeremy. I need to take a personal day." And hang up.

My boyfriend is gone before I'm off the phone, and I'm left to ponder the past few nights. Though fragmented memories and hallucinations cloud my thoughts, I realize I have a problem.

At the beginning of that weekend we'd planned—as we always planned— to stay sober for a change, but figured what the hell, it'd be cool to just do one more "bump" with a friend. That's all it ever took, a seemingly innocuous, miniscule mound of white powder on the end of a house key. If it had been salt, it would have been barely enough to make you sneeze, but it wasn't salt and it was enough to make us desperate for more.

Since we were trying to quit, we had already deleted all of our dealers' numbers and disconnected ourselves from most of our friends who still used drugs. Those we remained in touch with were regular users, and their dealers only sold large quantities. Since we were "small-timers," we were left to fend for ourselves. After a few unproductive phone calls, we opted for our last-ditch plan—to pick up a hooker on Polk Street and score a bag from her. So we drove to the Tenderloin District, up the street from our apartment, and parked our red BMW near the corner where the "girls" were standing.

"You lookin' to party, honey pie?" the tall Asian transsexual greeted me as I slowly approached. With a nervous grin I couldn't shake, I asked, "Do you know where I can find Tina?" That's what we called Crystal Meth. I read somewhere that someone started calling it that because you felt like a star when you started doing it, but after a few days you felt like Ike Turner beat your ass. The gays have a twisted sense of humor sometimes. Whatever the case, she knew what I was asking for and, with a subtle gesture from her fake green eyes, she directed me to her friend on her right.

I followed a small-framed white tranny around the corner to her building. She, like many of the "ladies," lived in a dingy, dilapidated hotel where we were greeted by an attendant behind a tall black steel cage. I could barely make out his silhouette in the shadows as we passed. She made a meaningful gesture in his direction and he said something inaudible back, but she knew the routine and led me up a few flights of stairs. The first door at the top was kicked into halves like a two-piece barn door, with the upper half closed and the lower half wide open and some guy's legs protruding into the hall. I stepped over him and wondered if he was alive. The shared bathroom on the left side of the corridor was vacant except for three cockroaches the size of small mice. The fluorescent light inside flickered like a disco strobe, and I cringed at the image of the roaches dancing on the walls.

"You sure this is all you want, honey?" she asked after handing me a small baggy filled with foggy shards of crystal. Her legs were long and thick as she leaned back onto her dresser and spread them slightly, seductively.

"I'm sure." I handed her a twenty and bolted out the door, not even making eye contact. I was too uncomfortable with the idea that I had just witnessed my life as an after-school special.

A decade spent in the unreal

That Monday morning was the first time I had ever really admitted that I had a problem. But it wouldn't be the last. I spent the next decade fading in and out of reality, reaching for something real in a world where everything seemed so out of reach. It seems impossible to make progress when all you've ever learned is how to survive. So I spent most of my life just barely making the money I needed to get by. As soon as I had what I needed, well... then it was time to get high. Even when I stopped using meth, there was always something else in its place.

Growing up, I had witnessed the ties between my adolescent mind and reality snap under the stress of my perception. Later I discovered things that whisked my senses even further from the logical. The first was when my cousin Jason, who was seven at the time, informed me out of the blue that we were brothers and that I had been adopted by my grandparents. The message was clear: everything I knew was a lie, and everyone who was nice to me had been hiding the truth all this time. Walking on the fragile surface of my mind, I fell through into the numbing embrace of my own insanity.

Turning away from the hands reaching out, I trusted no one.

Before I could even begin to grasp at the pieces of my fractured existence, the man I came to know as my father—the man, I had learned so abruptly, who was actually my grandfather—was taken to Genesee hospital, diagnosed with terminal lung cancer. The silent hand of cancer had swept across our lens, smearing it with mortality. Nothing mattered after that, because everything I knew was a lie and everyone I loved would eventually die.

They say that alcoholism is a disease that exists whether or not conditions dictate it. Good people from good homes drink to excess and find themselves in the dregs of their addictions. I often like to joke that finding out why I'm an alcoholic is akin to finding out why I'm gay. Even if I had the answer, I'd still crave the drink and the dick. So I don't spend too much time thinking about how I got to wherever I was. I chose to focus more on getting out of there.

Not feeling good... feeling *nothing*

The conditions of my life were not the reason I drank. They were the excuse, and being disconnected from reality at an early age only made it easier for me to distance myself further from life with drugs and alcohol. For most of my life I thought I used because it felt good, but I would eventually discover that I used so I wouldn't feel *anything*. Drugs and alcohol were my physical distraction from my emotional experience.

A part of me had almost always wanted to be free of everything life had to offer, all the lousy fucking things we just had to accept. Like loss and betrayal and death. I wanted to tell the universe that I wasn't going to play by the rules, so I fought the current and nearly drowned so many times I can't even count them. But then I noticed a theme common to every scene of desperation I experienced: no matter how hard I tried to die, I always survived.

I had spent my entire life too afraid to live and not quite hopeless enough to die, until the day I got the phone call I had been trying so hard to escape. It was my cousin, calling to tell me that my mom had just died. Suddenly the nonsense of my retreat from the life my mother had just lost stood up starkly, the way the ground seems to stand up when you fall.

I was at work when my cousin called, and my response was to drive to my best friend's house in a haze, unaware that my license had been suspended because of an accident a year before. My driving was erratic, so I got pulled over for running a red light. I told the officer about my recent loss, and he didn't arrest me, but he towed my car and told me I'd have to go see the sheriff in the morning to get it out of impound. I found out at the deputy station that there was a thirty-day hold on my car for driving with a suspended license. Thinking I was going to lose my car because I couldn't afford the fines, I pleaded with the deputy. He admitted he felt bad for me, but assured me there was little, if anything, he could do, saying he wanted "to check on something first."

The writing on the wall

I sat there in the station, freaked out by the possibility of losing my car right after losing my mom, and badly needing a distraction. My cell phone battery had died shortly after I got there, so I was left with nothing else to do but read a poem on the wall in front of me.

*In tears we saw you sinking
and watching you fade away,
our hearts were almost broken,
we wanted you to stay,
but when we saw you sleeping
so peacefully free from pain,
how could we wish you back
with us to suffer the pain again?
It broke our hearts to lose you
but you did not go alone,
for part of us was with you
the day God took you home.*

The poem was dedicated to a fallen police officer, and I read it dozens of times while I waited for the deputy to return. An hour passed before he came out with my driving record, saying, "There's nothing I can do. The law's pretty clear. The only person who can do anything is the supervisor on duty, but she never issues releases." He shook his head and looked at me apologetically. I held eye contact, but said nothing. I wasn't convinced he had done everything he could do. "But let me see what she says," he added.

I waited another hour, reading the poem another dozen times until the supervisor came out and asked, "Why were you driving with a suspended license?" I told her everything I could in the few minutes of her attention that I had. I told her that I was in recovery, that there was a lot of wreckage in my past, and that I had just lost my mom. With a discouraging look on her face, she shook her head and said, "Let me see what I can do."

Forty-five minutes later, the first deputy returned with my file. Meanwhile, I had probably read the poem another twenty times. The deputy shook his head and offered me some paperwork to sign. He then smiled and said, "You must have an angel on your shoulder, because she never signs releases."

But she had signed mine.

I didn't care. I just wanted out of there. I just had to get my car and somehow find the money I needed to get home for the funeral.

At the impound yard the attendant looked with puzzled disapproval when he asked, "What's this? I've never seen this form." I didn't care. I just wanted my car. I just wanted to see my family. "It's a release on my thirty-day hold," I offered, to his disbelief. "I'm going to have to call this in," he said, "I've never seen one of these." I was numb as I waited. Finally everything cleared and I got my car.

Friends at the gym where I worked and other trainers chipped in to help me get a flight. Late to the funeral, I rushed to the front of the church to sit with my brother. A third of the way up the aisle, I stopped, staring up at the final image in my mother's tribute. The background image on the projection screen was a sunset. My mom's picture took up the left column, and on the right were the words that halted my advance. I only needed to read a little past the first sentence, "In tears we saw you sinking/ and watching you fade away/ our hearts were almost broken..."

That was when it happened, my spiritual awakening. It felt like her breath, and it washed over me and through me until all I heard was a deep, penetrating whisper in my mind. I heard her say, "I love you," and suddenly, *I got it*. It was then that I saw myself through her eyes. I felt a love for myself that only a mother could feel for a son.

In death my mother was giving me that piece of her that I had always refused to accept.

At the funeral I realized that my life was not about all the failures, but was filled with lessons that I could use to prosper and grow. All I had to do was the opposite of what I had been doing, and instead of destruction I would create abundance.

Instead of dying, I chose life, and from that moment on everything changed for the better. I've learned to accept love in my life, because I've learned to accept my own love for myself.

I live every day as I would have if I were everything my mom ever wanted me to be.

Most important, I've realized that's exactly who I've always been.

About the Author

Jeremy B. Manning, Partner and Executive Producer at Vzn Studios, is a two-time International Bronze Medalist in Tae Kwon Do and a Master Trainer in Hollywood, California. Information about his personal training services can be found at TrainWithJeremy.com. Manning is also the host of the "Manning Up" radio show, where he talks with guests about using sports and fitness to overcome adversity. He is also the founder of ManningUpUSA.com, a resource for change through health, wellness, and recovery.

Part Two

The Power of "Yes"

The Memory in the Closet That Set Me Free

Kathleen Booker

"WHAT??!!"

My online banking statement had just appeared onscreen, showing my account overdrawn by a mysterious withdrawal in the amount of $21,833.

"Holy sh*t!" I said to myself, scratching my head. What did I do? How could I have incorrectly written a check for that amount? Now, bear in mind that I had NEVER written a five-figure check!!! That shows how deeply rooted in lack and scarcity I was.

Even worse, I had been languishing on the river of DE-NILE… munching on seeds of unconsciousness.

Now, this was not my first financial crisis. It was actually my third. *Nope, I lie.* It was my fourth. "Kathleen," the Universe was saying. "I am calling you… pick up your Life!"

I called the bank, fervently hoping it was a mistake, that it was really a deposit. Ha ha ha… oh gosh, I am my own source of constant amusement.

Face down, looking up for help

When the bank told me that the $21,833 was a lien against my account by a credit card collection agency, I threw myself on the floor, face down, and wailed to God that I needed help. I did not know what to do or how to do it and, more important, my husband was gonna kill me and how in the world could I tell him this!!??

That bank statement was one of many wake up calls I had received. What made this one different, however, was that this time I did pick up the phone and began the journey back to my Self.

My soul was crying out to be healed of many misbeliefs, including unworthiness, undeservedness, lack, scarcity, the idea of not being good enough and so on. My reaction to this episode showed that my human self was ready and willing to begin healing. I wondered, however, about where these misbeliefs came from. And how do I release them?

One of the things I know for sure is that when you ask the Universe for help, the Universe will always answer, though the answer will often surprise you.

So the journey to my Self began as I was led by still quiet voices to a Unity church, whose minister taught me the importance of having a consistent morning practice of prayer, journaling, and meditation. This is a practice I maintain to this day. Also, she taught Stretton Smith's 4 T Prosperity Course, a powerful program created by a Unity minister that deals with shifting and releasing from the mind old and non-supporting habits.

My consciousness began to expand when I became able to think in different ways. The minister also exposed me to the teachings of Science of Mind, as well as the Universal Laws and the Tao. I was learning how to free my mind from ancestral ties, ways of being and thinking that were not supporting my growth.

Yet money was still not flowing in my life.

Why the butterfly must struggle alone
During this time I was earning a so-called "living" as

an entrepreneur, holding on to a business that generated no income. I was determined to be a business owner, though I could not hold/grow the business. Sure, my business was a great idea, and in my core I knew it *could* work, but it was failing.

Picture a chrysalis in a cocoon, that's where I was. The chrysalis *must* open the cocoon itself, by stretching its wings. That action releases vital nutrients into its wings, to help it open up the cocoon and ultimately fly. Now imagine a well-meaning human coming along who sees the chrysalis and says, "Ooo let me help it open."

If that happens, and the butterfly is not allowed to do its work of stretching its wings, giving it the nutrients and strength to fly, it will come out of the chrysalis struggling without the nutrients it needs to thrive, to live, to fly... and ultimately dry up.

That was me... desiccated and floundering.

You know that saying, "Where you are is right where you are supposed to be"? Well, my response to hearing that was "Aarruugghhh." It was hard for me to hear. It was only in hindsight that I realized I had to learn to stretch my own wings, feeding myself nourishing nutrients of Truth, if I ever were to fly.

I kept moving forward as best I could, pulled by an unseen hand toward an unseen light and by quiet still voices. The journey did not feel good. However, I kept going because where I was, was so darn uncomfortable and miserable.

Feeling stymied, frustrated, impatient, and broke, I spoke with the minister, saying, "This ain't working. Where the hell is the money? Why aren't my relationships flourishing, why do I feel so uncomfortable in my own skin??!!" She suggested we have a "soul session." Desperate, I said yes.

During the session she asked me some questions. I really can't remember what they were, I just remember feeling terrible—sick, afraid... mortified. As she gently guided me, I remember wanting to shrink, to disappear, to do anything other than allow the memory that wanted to emerge to come all the way forward.

The healing power of an unwelcome memory

I did not want to remember it. I kept saying, "No, no, no I don't want to!"

Oh my God, even as I write this my heart is in my throat, and it's beating so fast.

But the minister didn't stop. She gently coaxed me to allow the memory to come forward. She asked me who I was "seeing," who was disturbing me so. I answered "My father." That brought up fear, terror, disgust, shame. Utter revulsion. I wanted to disappear entirely.

At that point my father had been dead over eight years, but apparently was still very much alive. What my soul was determined to bring to my conscious mind was the molestation by my father, which began when I was three months old.

"Oh my God!" I cried out to the minister, as I did my best to curl into a fetal position in the chair. 'What do I do with this?' She answered, "There is nothing to do, just be with it." I did not know what the hell that meant. My world had just ripped apart and I am to just *BE with it?*

For over a year I walked around pissed off at myself and the world, confused and attempting to find balance. I could not relate to my husband, and my marriage went through a rough time. I did muster the courage to tell him what came forth, and the saint that he is understood and supported me. That was very important, but it was still not enough. I was so baffled and enraged. *How does someone do that to a child??? What kind of sicko does shit like that?* I did not know what do, how to be, or how to get out of me all that I was feeling. "Aarruughhh!"

Again, the invisible hand and light came to lead me when I was told about Iyanla Vanzant's Wonder Woman Weekend.

What an awesome time that was... it revealed so much to me. I was able to find my voice that had been buried, allowing it to be heard. I knew I had to attend her school (Inner Visions Institute for Spiritual Development). I had no money, but I gave Iyanla $10 and told her put it on a seat with my name on it!

Uninvited lessons further the process
Just so you know, when I asked the Universe for healing, *everything I did NOT ask for* came forward to support me in my healing! Example: I got the Divine opportunity to heal another layer of lack, scarcity, and the misbelief that I am not enough, after I paid for my classes by cashing in stock my mother gave me, totally forgetting what I learned in Finance 101, that I would have to pay taxes on my realized gains from cashing in the stocks!

I remember when our tax return was confiscated by the IRS as payment, and I thought *Oh shit... God, can ya cut a sistah a break?* My husband (the saint) said, "Kathleen, your choices affect not just you, you affect both of us, because we are a team." My mother was also disappointed that I cashed in the stock. All this offered me a Divine opportunity to begin healing the codependent relationship I had with my mother and to continue healing my relationship with my husband!

What I came to see was that all of these "incidences" in my relationships were an outpicturing of the defenses, misbeliefs, and barriers I had created as a way to survive the molestation.

My studies at Iyanla's Inner Visions Institute included an introduction to Conscious Connected Breathing. That practice brought forward even more of the molestation memories. I had buried them so deeply, but now I was beginning to disentangle my true Self, one breath at a time.

Abundance—and breath—begin to flow
After Inner Visions I noticed that money began to flow at an infinitesimally higher rate. I did get a "real" job in order to support myself and become fiscally responsible. Breathwork allows a fast-forward healing, so I began working with some of the masters of Breathwork to accelerate my healing and continue my growth.

I also found my Purpose: to spread the power of the Breath.

The breath is so powerful that the act of surrendering to it allowed me to release the guilt, pain, shame, and fear I had surrounded the molestation memories with. Only then was I able to breathe life, joy, and peace into my life, releasing lack, scarcity, and the feeling of being not enough. I breathed it all away and breathed in the truth of who I am: the Divine Beloved Daughter of the Most High... the Daughter in whom He is well pleased.

With every Breath I took my innocence back.

Life is a journey, and I have more roads to travel. But I am far from where I was before. Thank You, God! I have a peace I heretofore never had. It is delicious and delightful. I am continuing to be financially responsible, and my relationships are thriving.

I have released a whole lot of anger toward my father, anger that only ate *me* up. It was like taking poison and expecting someone else to die. In one of my Breathwork sessions my father came forward and apologized. I do forgive him. In another Breathwork session my father told me he himself had been abused, not that that makes the molestation OK, but as my Spiritual teacher says, he did the best he could with what he knew at that time. Now it is up to me. Not only have I been able to heal my relationship with my father, he is now an Angel I feel around me, supporting me through life.

As trite as it sounds, life is a journey, not a destination... one breath at a time.

Deep breath!

I can say it now: *Right where I am is right where I am supposed to be...* breath-fully Blessed!

About the Author

Kathleen Booker is quite passionate about Breathwork, knowing first-hand the energy, peace, and joy it creates in one's life. A certified Conscious Connected Breathwork Coach who has worked with many masters in that field, she offers Conscious Connected Breathwork meditation workshops to individuals and senior citizen centers, hospices, colleges and other groups. Feeling that giving back to the community is imperative, she has given her time and talents to the Alzheimer's Association and Village Care of New York, an AIDS/HIV Day Treatment Program. She is also a Big Sister, connected to several neighborhood youth groups, and serves as a motivational speaker for organizations, small-business development groups, and motivational workshops. She is a certified Spiritual Coach and certified Giver of Oneness Blessing, and is reachable through her website at Kathleen@BreathingForFreedom.com.

So Much Air, So Little Time

Pamela Holtzman

This is a time of reflection for me—call it an inventory of my past sixty years.

At this moment, I am in paradise, on retreat at our home in the Bahamas. This singular place was created through serendipity and courage, built in good faith in the wake and aftermath of the devastation of September 11, 2001. I frequently take refuge in the healing waters and breezes of this island, casting off the stress and brutalities of the other world. I use retreat time to disappear from my daily life, to be with nature, shedding, allowing to come up whatever needs to come up, to let go of whatever needs to go.

When I was younger, I could witness deterioration and disintegration and identify it as the human condition, but I couldn't identify *with* it. Bestowed with the gifts of health and energy, I thought I was immortal. After all, I was a twenty-three-year-old top fashion model, the mother of a beautiful baby girl, with a wonderful husband.

Mine was an idyllic life, and it felt like an eternal one.

The idyll ended when I started developing odd pains that would snake up my back, debilitating fatigue, and a slow strangulation of my airways. I was hospitalized with what appeared to be a cyst on my neck that was squeezing my windpipe. It turned out to be stage IV non-Hodgkin's lymphoma.

I had been given a death sentence, just when my adult life was beginning. I was only twenty-three.

I lived through the "lifetime" dose of radiation and a clinical trial of chemo. Thinking I wouldn't need it, doctors removed my spleen, only to learn later that it is an essential organ for strengthening the immune system, especially useful in fighting pneumonitis. Nobody seemed to know the long-term effects of any of my treatments. All I knew was that I was alive, and from then on I was bent on making every moment count!

The crisis after the crisis

Every crisis has its aftershock; for years, mine left me gasping for breath with respiratory illnesses. Fighting back, I breathed, meditated, and swam religiously, in an effort to reclaim my strong, healthy body, until at last I felt the rivers of vitality starting to flow again. I felt renewed, revived, returned to health.

Despite my restored strength, however, I was still left with the memento of scar tissue, the reminders of many assaulted and wounded places. My lifetime of struggles and effort had resulted in a body strong in structure, but viscerally weak. For years I was in and out of the hospital, being treated for bowel obstructions. My answer was to live in full survival mode. All I needed was hydration and decompression, and I was back living my good full life—until the next incident.

These traumatic relapses recurred seven times in seven years, until my body just wouldn't let go, and that last scar, that final grief, needed to be cut out.

After that final surgery my body was at peace for a while.

Later, scar tissue, one of the effects of radiation, claimed space in my lungs, compromising my immune system, making me vulnerable to viruses, antigens, and bacteria that could stress the delicate network of tissue, forever reminding me of my vulnerability, my humanness.

Becoming lighter, organ by organ

Then one day the earth herself got me. Red Dust, Coccodidiomycosis, Valley Fever, all are names for the next culprit. I was so sick that my lungs became lakes of fluid, and I was gripped with fever and pain. This illness wasn't even on the medical radar for a Midwesterner, until the doctors began to consider my recent trip to Arizona as a source. The endless parade of scans and probes ultimately located a tumor on my left kidney. Though only ten percent of kidney tumors are benign, mine was. I left the hospital with one kidney and, to treat the original problem, a six-month supply of antifungal medication.

First my spleen, then one kidney—I was getting lighter, organ by organ! I retreated to my island to heal and swim in the ocean waters. Bathing in warm salt water lifted the redness from my newly scarred belly, and I healed once again.

I have a hunger for the sea and sky, which I satisfy by retreating to our little island. The salt water provides healing at every level, while swimming in the ocean returns me to the womb. Breathing while I'm in the water, where my body is weightless and strong, comes as second nature to me. The island winds are like a hyperbaric chamber of extra oxygen and ions that charge my cells and tissues. I heal here, where nature provides me the space to be present with myself, to receive what I need.

Here is where I recover the well of resilience that I need in the face of adversity, the well that keeps the vibrant life force of my body moving in the direction of healing.

But where does this resilience come from? One answer lies in my understanding that I have the power to determine my response to any situation. I access that power through both internal and external awareness, and through my curiosity about what's going on, what I can do about it, and how to go through it. I explore with a sense of wonder without fear, finding a purpose for it all.

I learned that the power of the mind and our beliefs can either heal or create more pain and suffering, can cure or kill. I was fascinated by that concept, so I gave myself permission to cultivate my positive imagination. I realized that with every practice and choice I made I was fighting for the ability to imagine the world I wanted to create, in which I would experience a healthier, happier life. I wanted to understand psychology, and how the mind/body link affects well being and potential healing.

I knew from my own experience how positive

thinking, affirmations, and practicing joy changed my life. I knew that all those things, combined with many prayers and connecting with my spirit, made powerful medicine.

Without my early cancer experience to "wake me up" to really engaging positively in life, I might have stayed stuck in my delusionary vision of who I was supposed to be. Now *all* of my practices are my life's work; they define what I do, and who I am.

Today I understand that my soul is what makes me unique; it's my personal life force, which shapes the content and the form of the lessons in my life. My soul keeps me connected to what I feel and learn from my body and from nature. It's my soul that keeps me alive.

The only survivor from my survivors' group

From the moment of my diagnosis at such a young age, I felt compelled to teach directly from my experience, perhaps because I was attempting to articulate to myself what was happening. In my "early cancer days," I teamed up with three other women from our support group, which we named "Make Today Count." We gave lectures to high school students and did radio shows, discussing our experiences of living with the sentence of "death by cancer."

Within a year, the other three women had passed away.

When I realized I was the only one left from the group, I became obsessed with the need to understand more about death and dying. I had a driving desire to go deeper in my exploration. I returned to school to get my nursing degree; all I wanted to do was hospice work. Being a handmaiden to death humbled me and taught me in many profound ways: to not fear the imminence of death, but to realize that the real work of dying is living fully; to appreciate the importance of being honest and open with loved ones; to know how to receive and let go; and to recognize the essential and universal need to love and be loved.

After ten years of hospice work, I was ready to expand upon my understanding of death, and finally ready to dig in to the living! Retiring from nursing, I spent many years working with the Cancer Wellness Center, Northbrook, Illinois, where I taught classes, sharing the meditation and visualization tools I had found to be paramount in my own healing process. Our group grew and became a community as we supported each other through unknown territory, each of us sharing a piece of our story and, in return, enriching and inspiring one another along the way. It was a gift to be a part of the founding days of this unique facility.

Starting with nothing, twenty-five years ago, today the center not only serves thousands of people with cancer, but their significant others as well. It was in this environment that I grew professionally, giving birth to the Healthy Lifestyle Program for survivors. Until then there had been no blueprint telling us how to move forward while staying well. It was my challenge to put all my practices and knowledge about health into a simple form, to help others take the healthy path, and stay there.

Free-falling into the great unknown

I've cultivated a credo for how to live my life without regrets. First, I want to live my own life, not a life that's expected by others. I'm intent on maintaining a balance, as I work hard and play hard. I always speak my truth and express my feelings (at least to myself!), and I make an effort to maintain my connection with friends and family. This is the way I live my life with joy.

As I continued to explore the vital mind/body connection, my degree in social work opened more doors and opportunities to learn and explore wellness, deepening and integrating health into my own life. Honing the concept of a healthy lifestyle into a form that I could teach and share with so many, I began to see my purpose come full circle.

When I survived cancer, I made a choice to live the best way I possibly could, for as long as I was able. I know I am here to somehow make a difference in the lives of others. I envision my hand reaching down to lift up many others, as so many hands have reached down and lifted me. I have an awareness that my work in healing myself is my contribution to the healing of the world.

There is no guarantee of health for me or anybody else, I am fully aware of that. What my practice of healthy living does is to provide me with the best resources, enabling me to function optimally, meeting the needs of my body and my soul. My personal rewards are strength, flexibility, nourishment, restful sleep, peace, gratitude, and joy.

I do know *to trust* that perfection underlies everything, without needing to understand anything else. Life happens, changes occur, transitions evolve, and all of a sudden I find myself free-falling into the Great Unknown. I'm excited, and ready, for whatever life delivers next.

I am a peaceful warrior-in-waiting. As Joseph Campbell said, "We must be willing to let go of the life we've planned, so as to have the life that is waiting for us."

About the Author

Upon receiving a diagnosis of life-threatening cancer in her early twenties, Pamela Holtzman, RN, LCSW, began an in-depth study of the various components of daily living that optimize her goal of having a healthy lifestyle through healthy eating, daily meditation, regular exercise, and cultivating a practice of having a clear mind and an open heart. With deep compassion, patience, and wisdom, Pamela shares her knowledge with others so they, too, can experience a more balanced and happy life. Pamela began her professional career as a registered nurse, caring for patients in hospice. She has spent the majority of her twenty-five-year career as a psychotherapist, certified wellness practitioner, public speaker, and workshop facilitator. Pamela is the author of *The Healthy Lifestyle Path of Wellness,* a comprehensive reference guide based on the author's experiences, for anyone looking to enhance day-to-day living through mind, body, and soul healing on a foundation of balance and harmony. Visit PamelaHoltzman.com

The Journey Home

Margaret-Mary Kelly

I had just been journaling the day before about my life and the quandary I was in. I was excited to start my pottery class. I had received a scholarship and was quite thrilled to be with such great artists, especially since I had not sat in a class since I was a young child. It was late, about nine-thirty p.m. when I returned home from class. My then-boyfriend had left a message inviting me over to visit friends. Stupidly, in love, I went.

I was awakened the next morning by the phone ringing at seven a.m. It was my oldest sister. We had all been sitting vigil in our own ways as we awaited the news from hospice about our other sister, Kathy, who was dying of pancreatic cancer.

I should mention that I was exhausted, having just returned from a trip to San Francisco. So my sister Anne Marie says, "This looks like the day. You had better get down to visit her today if you want to see her one last time." Anne Marie lives in Vermont and can not come today; our brother, Donny, is working in California, and Dad is living about two hours away.

It is a two-and-a-half-hour drive to hospice each way. This is like going to the dentist for me. We are not a close family. I had not spoken to my sister Kathy in about five years, until we found out about this diagnosis in July, 2012. Now I am to babysit a friend's kids at noon, and I still have to go home and shower before that. I think I clocked 500 miles that day, all within Connecticut.

But yes, I guess I can go down to the hospice. I would only stay for an hour at a time, this is all I can handle. After all, Kathy and I had not talked for so many years. I am not ready to be best friends again, and am really not even sure this diagnosis is for real, either.

The undeserving sister

Over the years I've had to remove myself from some of the people around me because of their mental health and addiction issues, and I was not able to deal with my sister's drug addiction or fake health problems, as she vied for attention, any longer. Back in 1988 she told me she had a brain tumor so I would feel sorry for her and have her in my wedding party. It worked. I did have her as a bridesmaid. She was miraculously healed a year later. Hmm.

This time I am not going to waste time and energy if this is another false plea for attention, plus a little hypochondria. OK, I realize that a month prior she overdosed and a call to 911 had brought her back and she was in the hospital for a week or two. So maybe this time it's for real. But I am still skeptical.

So I go down to see her that afternoon. I walk in the room and my dad is going through her belongings on the other side of the bed and his girlfriend is holding her hand and Kathy is asleep and looks really bad. OK I believe her now.

"Hi Kathy," I whisper softly in her ear as I give her a kiss on the cheek. She wakes up and says, "Oh Mimi, you came back from California. How was the trip?" I am shocked at how quickly she went downhill in just ten days.

Before I left on my trip I visited her and bought her some Italian Ice and a Big Mac and French fries. Now she is flat out and can barely move. Joan gets up so I can sit next to Kathy, and I hold her hand while she just dozes and smiles.

We are all leaving, since we know we are going to hit bad traffic on I-95 the closer it gets to five o'clock. Kathy does not like it when we all leave. She has a tear running from her left eye down her cheek almost in slow motion.

An unforgettable tear
It all hits me. Kathy is really sick and really going to die. I decide to let Dad have time with her and I leave first, because I cannot stay any longer. I have the dog with me in the car, so I walk him on the beach where we see the huge waves and feel the strong wind. It is cleansing and so pretty there.

So, two-and-a-half more hours on the highway. All the way home my thoughts are of that tear running down Kathy's cheek as we said good bye, and I have this nagging feeling of "Turn around, go back." But a bad storm is coming, with hurricane-type winds and rain. So I keep heading home.

I get back home, feed the dog, and I so want to take a nap, but I have to meet some friends. I get back home again finally about nine-thirty or ten p.m., and soon I'm in bed.

But the memory of that tear keeps popping back into my head. Should I go back down to Branford, two hours away?

The rain is pounding outside, the wind is howl-ing. The storm has begun. I'm so tired and I do not know what to do. So I sit up in bed and the phone rings. My friend Sandy is saying, "Why don't you just call the nurse and check on her?" Oh yeah, thanks, Alexander Graham Bell. I forgot about that great in-vention: the telephone! But I am one not to bother nurses. They have busy jobs. So I thank Sandy for the advice, figuring I'll make the call anyway and then sleep better. I call down there and they patch me through to Kathy's nurse. I am on hold for a while. The person answering the phone asks who I am and I say "Her sister," and then I'm on hold again till some-one picks up and says, "Oh, hi Anne Marie." I say, "No, this is her little sister."

The nurse is amazed—she'd never heard of me. I say, "We were not close." She reports that Kathy is very fitful tonight and restless and cannot sleep. She tells me Kathy said she was scared.

OK, that does it. I lose it. The tear, the feeling of Turn Around and Go Back, and now I hear she is afraid. I MUST go. I tell the nurse, "I am on my way! Please tell Kathy I will be there by midnight." I also ask how the storm is down there on the coast, and the nurse says she has no idea because she is inside on a double shift. I thank her for caring for my sister and ask her name. She says, " I am Gwen." That's really it, I start crying. My oldest daughter has the same name. I know this, too, is another sign.

Ok, so here we go, out in this wicked windy night,

back down to Branford, me and my dog. I put his dog bed in the back seat and pack some bones and hope for the best. I also bring my laptop, though I do not know why, at this point. I put on some really peaceful Sanskrit music and pray the entire length of the drive.

Calling in the seen and unseen

I arrive at midnight. Something tells me to bring in my laptop and the CD from the car stereo. If this is really the night she is passing, we're going to be needing all the help we can get. I learned from an Aboriginal Shaman that it takes a lot of energy to leave the body, and I knew how tired and weak Kathy was just hours earlier. So I think about the waves and the wind and the rain and all the energy of the storm. Maybe that is why I am not scared. I am supposed to feel this enormous energy and soak it in, to use it for Kathy.

I get to her room as the nurse is helping her roll over. I walk in and lean over and say, "Kathy, I am here." She says, "Oh Mimi, you must be sooo tired!" I say, "Don't worry, I am here for you, you don't have to be scared any more, you are not alone." She looks at me with the eyes of a little child and says, "You won't leave?" I say, "No, I will stay here with you as long as you need me to, except to go to the bathroom, of course." She laughs and says. "OK, that's allowed."

She tells me it's been hard to sleep and she cannot relax. She asks me to help her relax. I say, "Let's pray." All of a sudden words I have not uttered in

101

decades come streaming out of my mouth, just as they did when Kathy would help me by praying with me when I was scared at night in the bedroom we shared growing up.

I begin, "Now I lay me down to sleep. I pray the Lord my soul to keep…" I gasp as I realize what the next line would be, and swallow the lump in my throat. She is calming down. I continue, "If I should die before I wake…" My lips are quivering and tears are bursting out of my eyes from cells I never knew I had before. I take a huge deep breath and finish the prayer with her. She seems not to notice the words. Thank God.

" I pray the Lord my soul to take."

I quickly add, " Remember you always said that one with me when I was little?" She laughs. We both laugh. I say, "What else do you want to pray?" She holds up her hand and she is gripping Rosary beads so tightly I know she has been really scared.

I am very glad I am here. I say, "OK, let's say the Rosary," though I have NEVER said a complete Rosary in my entire life, Catholic or not (God forgive me). I am so worried that I would not do it "right," but I figure I would get points for the effort and we could just figure it out as we went along, or not.

As it turns out, we say the entire thing. There must be Divine power working here, because I believe we said it correctly. Maybe all that Catechism actually sunk in. Then we laugh at some old memories about going to Catholic school and cheerleading and our dogs.

Kathy is quite coherent at this time. She dozes off every so often and I sit there and hold her hand and rub her arm. She wakes and asks for ginger ale and I get her some. She says she wants some Italian ice, so I go down the hall to the freezer to get her one. I know I bought her Italian ice before I went to California, and when I was putting them away in the same freezer I wrote her name on them, and a man nearby looked at me with a funny look. Noticing that I had bought about three boxes for her, he said, "My, we are quite hopeful."

I now reach for an ice, the auspicious one, the only one left.

I feed Kathy a few spoonfuls of cherry ice and some sips of ginger ale. She is like a little baby now, totally contented as I wipe her mouth. She rests. I rest next to her. When I think she's sleeping I answer a text from that boyfriend, and Kathy looks up at me as clear as day and says, "What are you doing?" I am caught like a school kid chewing gum. I say, "I'm sorry, I was texting." Kathy gets a look on her face as if to say, "How dare you not pay attention to me, hello I'm dying here!" We both laugh again. I put my phone away.

She says, "Please help me relax again." I tell her I had brought some music and could play it on my computer. Though the other patients are unconscious, it actually might help all of us. So I quietly play some yoga music, Sanskrit chants. It helps me feel peaceful too.

Kathy's words are down to one-word statements.

She says, "nurse," and I call the nurse. She says "priest." The nurse tells me Kathy already received the Last Rites, but she would see what she could do.

A strangely comforting mystery voice
Now Kathy is really not even saying words. She just lifts her finger and I know she wants to press her button for pain relief. I press it. She sleeps. The nurse tells me they cannot find a priest at this time of night, but they have someone on the phone who can talk with us and pray with us. So they patch the call through. I answer and place the phone near our ears so we can both hear this praying voice. I explain to the woman on the phone that Kathy is in transition, that she is scared and wants a priest.

The voice on the phone says she is so happy she can be with us at this special time and thinks it's wonderful for us to have each other at this time. Her praying voice is so comforting, so soft, so warm and so familiar, it reminds me of safe, loving arms. This woman never tells me her name or what church she is from. Kathy is smiling like a baby being rocked by her mama. We listen as the woman on the phone says the 23rd Psalm. *The Lord is my shepherd...* I take deep breaths and hold back tears again and recite as best I can and Kathy becomes a baby being told a bedtime story.

I thank the woman and hang up the phone. All of a sudden *crash, boom bang,* things are falling, a water bottle, a fan, and I don't know what else are falling to the floor, and I am shaking my head. I am on the other side of the room and Kathy is unable to move, but something is happening without us.

The nurse comes in to check on the commotion, and I tell her I did not know how things got spilled and dropped. She and I clean everything up.

Weird!

The nurse is not fazed, saying "Things happen." I only put a meaning to this event later on. After reviewing the day with my daughter Julia on the phone from California, she comforts me, saying "I'm sorry your sister died. Maybe she just needed to be with your mom."

My mom. My MOM! Julia's saying that goes off like the lights in Times Square. The mystery voice on the phone was so familiar, yet I knew I hadn't heard it in so long. It had been thirty-two years since I had heard Mom's voice.

The voice on the phone sounded like my mother.

Kathy and I had once made an agreement that she would try to communicate after she died to let us know she was there, by flicking the lights or knocking something over. Maybe our mother heard that agreement and knocked those things over to let us know *she* was there.

We are so connected. Kathy and I were holding hands with our mother as she passed thirty-two years ago, and I feel my mom was there to help me when Kathy passed.

You can let go, because I will not
The nurse helps Kathy into a new position, checks her tubes, and I go out for more coffee. When Kathy dozes off again I am startled awake by the sound of her breath changing. Now it's like gasping. I call the nurse. It seems Kathy's lungs are filling with fluid or collapsing. The nurse comes and makes her more comfortable again.

The last thing my sister says to me before she stops talking is, "Thank you." I say "No. I thank *you*." When she looks at me quizzically, I say, "For the privilege of letting me be here with you now. I love you." She mouths, "Love you." We had made amends and talked about being sisters. She said I was a nice sister. I said I was sorry for not being a better friend.

Now her eyes are changing too. They seem very wide, as though they can see far. And they are clear, like her skin, which doesn't have a wrinkle on it or a blemish or a freckle. Her hands have an ivory softness, like a china doll, so precious. I set the CD to play the chanting. I love this music. It is called "The Journey Home."

My big sister and I look in each other's eyes and breathe to the rhythm of the music. I reminisce with her about fun times when we were little, swimming in Gramma's pool and floating on rafts. Her eyes get bigger.

Now as we breathe she often gasps. I know it's getting harder for her to breathe, so I remind her to relax and let God help. God could hold her in his arms and God could breathe for her. This seems to make it easier. I say, "Feel God's arms" as we breathe and she says *God*, and I say, "Feel the love all around you" and she says *Love*. I say "Daddy loves you" and she replies *I love Daddy*. I name all the people I can think of here on Earth that she knew and all the ones who have passed and she says she loves them. I tell her our mom is waiting for her with open arms. She responds *I love Mommy*.

Her breath changes again and is even softer and more shallow, like a fish out of water. I say, "Just feel the love" and we look at each other and breathe to the music of OM. Our eyes lock. It's as if I can read her mind, as if I know exactly what her body is doing. I can feel the tightness of her chest taking in less and less air as her eyes get bigger and clearer.

Whatever she can see, she is getting closer to it.

I breathe and she breathes. Once again I say, "Just let God breathe for you," and she utters a huge gasp and says *GOD*. She is smiling, and there's the brightest bling in her eyes, like the sparkle of a diamond, bright as all the stars brought together at once, so pure, clean, and clear.

It shoots out from her in all directions and she goes. She *goes*.

I know I've just seen my sister seeing God.

That is the most amazing thing I have ever experienced, along with the birth of my children. Thank you, dear sister. Thank you, dear God.

As I sit watching Kathy's body, the room slowly lightens up. Dawn is breaking, the sun is rising on the new day. The rising sun is shining through the window onto Kathy's face. A golden light is bathing my sister in angelic beauty. She is an angel now.

All this time I am holding her hand. I told her I would not let go and I kept my promise.

The nurse tells me she checked her vital signs and yes, it is true. I leave the Rosary beads in her hands and go out to walk on the beach. The waves are gone. I have never seen the ocean like this before, like glass. No wind. I feel so still, so surreal.

My daughter Gwynne calls me and I tell her to please always make friends with her sister, Julia, before it is too late.

I cry.

I look down in the grass and there is a four-leaf clover.

About the Author

Born in Brooklyn, New York, Margaret-Mary Kelly was raised in Connecticut. She is the mother of two daughters, one based on each coast, and is an artist, a craftsperson, and a gardener living in Connecticut's Litchfield Hills. "The Journey Home" is a chapter from her memoir-in-progress.

From Anxiety to ASSET:

A Teen's Journey

Tessa Zimmerman

Midnight. School night. Homework finished, but it's never good enough. I'm never good enough.

Tears stream down my cheeks as I stare blankly at my textbooks. I can feel it coming: the uncontrollable shaking, the pain in my chest, the lump in the back of my throat, the hyperventilating. Then the awful thought, "You are going to fail..." That single idea sends me over the edge and I am gone.

I scream as loud as I can, anything to get some help. My hands shake, and then the shaking spreads across my entire body, even affecting my breath, until I feel completely out of control. I try to catch my breath, but it's too rapid and harsh. The thoughts in my head scream, "You're going to fail... you're never going to amount to anything... your entire life depends on tomorrow's test." I close my eyes, hoping to escape this new panic attack.

That was then.

Today I am a confident, resilient, seventeen-year-old entrepreneur, while only four years ago I was crippled by that level of severe anxiety and panic attacks, an obsessive-compulsive disorder, post-traumatic stress disorder, and depression.

This is my story

I have been told that I cried for the entire first year of my life. If this wasn't a sign that I was going to be an anxious child, I don't know what was. I can clearly remember having panic attacks in the classroom and at home, from eight years old on. Up until then my life was full of a healthy desire for learning, and I loved the idea that school was a place dedicated

111

to learning. The more knowledge I gained, the more fulfilled I was. I just wanted to know everything, and that's where the trouble began. Because if I thought I wasn't able to know everything, that I wasn't able to be "perfect," my only option was to fall apart.

This is how it felt:
I am sitting at my school desk, staring at my writing assignment. I look around the room and everyone is working, except for me. The obsessive thoughts start and grow louder. "You are not good enough... you can't write, but everyone else can." I want those thoughts to go away. I close my eyes tight in an attempt to hold back the tears.

With the anxiety rising, I try to get help from my teacher, so I follow her around, her unwanted shadow. I can see her getting tense as her shadow nears her. I know she hates me. I know she can't stand to have me in her class, but I just want to be helped so badly. When I ask her for help, she ushers me back to my seat, as if all I needed was an escort. I see more and more students handing in their work, so I try to pretend to be working. I move my pencil across the paper.

I try to be the student I want to be—the one who can get through a class without freaking out. But I am not that student. So I do what I do best: panic. Once again I start to shake, tears roll down my cheeks, and then I can't catch my breath. As I am clearly disrupting the class, my teacher ushers me out of the room and into the hall. I want to be mad at her, to show her that she can prevent this by offering me support, instead of pushing me away.

But she sends me to the assistant principal with my writing assignment in hand.

This episode happens daily during my third-grade year, during which I am not taught any lesson but one: that having panic attacks is what problem children do. I am punished every time I have such an attack in class. I am a problem child.

As the years pass, my anxiety is never tackled head on, so I never learn how to handle this disorder that I have been so blessed with. I don't know how to calm myself down when I feel the panic rising, since I have been given no coping mechanisms except to push my anxiety to the side till I get home. This lack of self-control would later tear me apart during my middle school years.

Crowded hallways, screaming teachers, constant quizzes, locker jams, this is a description of my hell. Every time I enter those school doors, I feel as if a giant starving tiger is running toward me. My body has the same adrenaline reaction to school as it does to any serious threat.

It's no wonder I am so afraid of school, after my series of negative encounters with both teachers and classmates. I am pretty sure the idea behind giving students "extra help" is for students to actually receive extra help, but it isn't so for me. Instead, I get yelled at for asking for clarifications and am told, "Tessa I am not your tutor, stop asking so many questions." I become so afraid of my teachers that I am unable to learn at all, so my parents hire a tutor to help me survive middle school. I learn more in an hour with a tutor than I would in a week of school. Why is this? It is because I feel safe.

Because I am an "A" student, the school system doesn't care less how I get the grades. They don't care that every night I am killing my emotional well-being with my obsession about being their perfect student. It doesn't matter that for two years I have had panic attacks every night till one in the morning, or that I can't sleep because I am afraid of what the next day might bring. My parents try to get the school system to help me, but they are told just to put me on medication. That's all they can do: drug me into functioning.

Parents at their wit's end
My parents do everything they can to help me battle my anxiety. One thing they try is a therapist. Being the obsessive-compulsive person that I am, even a therapist's office with algae growing in the fish tank puts me on edge. The therapist talks for most of the time, my parents talk for the rest of the time, and I stare at the algae. Each therapy session leaves me more anxious, so I conclude that it is a pointless waste of time when I could be studying valuable information that would determine my success in life (or at least that's what the school system leads me to believe). Studying for my next test is way more important than therapy. However, my father disagrees, taking all my textbooks, flashcards, notes,

and throwing them into the back seat of the car. As I dive in to retrieve my books, he closes the car door. Before I know it he is backing out of the driveway, and I am on my way to another failed attempt at a therapy session.

One day, after emphasizing my need for help to the guidance counselor, I come home to find a voice-mail message from that same counselor: "Take Tessa to Hall Brook." Hall Brook is a mental hospital. My heart drops to the pit of my stomach, and I cry.

I think everyone comes to a profound moment in his or her life. This was my moment. Though the pain seemed unbearable, it was that pain that told me I had to make a change. It was then I realized that my suffering with overwhelming emotions and fears at that time was no indication that I was going to feel that way forever. I was so young and had (and still do) my whole life ahead of me. My story wasn't yet completely written. *I was in charge of my life.* I knew there were other options besides school. There were techniques out there, coping mechanisms for just such anxieties as mine. I just hadn't learned them yet, but that didn't mean I wouldn't. For the first time, I understood that my life was mine to live.

"Tessa, get out of the car."
"Mom, I can't. I just can't."
We are parked outside of Easton Country Day School. It's my second day of school as an official student there. I don't know why, but I am so afraid.

I keep seeing the images of my old school and the teachers I feared. I stare at the new school and cry. I want so badly to be able to enter the building happy and unafraid. But I can't escape my anxious thoughts. My mother leaves the car, determined to get me through those school doors.

I see the director, Mrs. Inwood, coming out of the school. The familiar intense fear rises as she nears the car. Then she does something I do not expect—she gets into the driver's seat of our car! It's empty because my mom is going for a walk.

"What is this woman doing?" My mind is blown as Mrs. Inwood leans over and gives me a hug. Next she asks me what I'm feeling. Nobody has ever asked me that. No one has ever cared about how I felt. They were only concerned with my grades. Mrs. Inwood tells me I am safe and, though I am hesitant, I believe her. Her hug alone tells me that somehow I know she's going to take care of me. We get out of the car together, and I am in the building.

My anti-anxiety tools
There's a technique to living with anxiety. For twelve years I was unaware of what to do when I felt anxious, until I met Mrs. Inwood and her daughter, Jamie. With their help, I started to live again. When I say "live," I simply mean the ability to perform the everyday tasks of a student with less anxiety. For instance, Jamie taught me how to tackle my homework in a way that wouldn't cause me to panic. Mrs. Inwood targeted activities that helped to calm my body when

I felt on the verge of panicking. Slowly but surely I gained more and more of my life back.

Then, just as I was beginning to reintroduce myself to school, life threw me a curve ball when I was diagnosed with Lyme disease, which comes from a tick bite and has both neurological and physical affects. Some days I couldn't straighten my elbows because it was too painful. I would stare at my elbows and cry. It was as if I could *see* their pain. Since the antibiotics made it difficult to keep food down, I lost a significant amount of weight within a few months.

Life seemed to keep on throwing up brick walls.

The brick walls are there for a reason. The brick walls are not there to keep us out. The brick walls are there to give us a chance to show how badly we want something. Because the brick walls are there to stop the people who don't want it badly enough. They're there to stop the other people.
Randy Pausch, *The Last Lecture*

Then, all of a sudden, the brick walls started collapsing faster than I could have ever imagined. I was finally starting to feel safe in school, with the help of my new "bodyguard," Nathan, who was there to take me out of the classroom whenever I felt a panic attack coming on, before I lost control. I started to discover other ways that would help me to have a better handle on my anxiety; fitness and nutrition were two of the ways. Instead of letting my anxiety build, I learned to work it off through physical activity. I found what foods made me anxious and others that calmed my body. I gained a wonderful Mindfulness teacher, Miss Casey, who taught me how to become aware of my anxious patterns through meditation. On my own, I began to develop coping tools designed specifically for me.

I came to the realization that if I, a struggling teen, found these methods helpful, then maybe others would find them helpful too. So I started a blog called "TeenSanity," as a way to share my journey of healthy living with others. I didn't expect anyone to read it. But as I began to write, I found I had a love of sharing my knowledge with others. I began to find my voice, the voice I had lacked for so much of my childhood, when I hadn't been able to speak my feelings or even acknowledge them. Now I was able to accept my struggles and use my experience to help others. That was powerful.

Everything that I had gone through finally seemed worth it, because I was able to see that the rewards were so much grander than the struggle.

Life at a place of no limits

There's an edge where the Pacific Ocean meets the sky, where the two almost combine into one, creating a sense of infinity. I stare at the bright blue Hawaiian sky, amazed that I am able to travel here without my parents. I am on an island, a twelve-hour plane ride away, and this is the first time I will be away from home longer than a couple of nights. I spend the days snorkeling and playing with sea turtles, while my nights are spent lying face up on the driveway, admiring the star-filled Hawaiian sky. I have never felt so independent. As I stare at the infinite Pacific, I hear the message that I am going to go into business. An overwhelming feeling of *There's More I Can Do* sweeps over my body. I smile with this newfound idea. I know how I can help the world: by empowering teenagers to become their best selves. I don't know how I am going to do this, but I know I will.

That moment was the beginning of ASSET.

Today I help teenagers realize and enable their potential using my own model. ASSET stands for

- Awareness
- Self-Efficacy
- Science of Happiness
- Exploration, and
- Touch and Connection.

I believe these five categories represent the skills teenagers need in order to better both themselves and the world.

- **Awareness** (or Mindfulness), enabled me to identify my anxiety triggers, and then I was able to use that knowledge to master my own anxiety.

- **Self.** Building a toolbox of coping mechanisms enabled me, not only to survive, but to thrive, even during times of anxiety.

- Coming out of a bleak world, I realized that there was a bit of **Science** as well as a few tricks to learn when it came to gaining happiness.

- Anxiety often made me close-minded, and

not until I was able to open my mind and **Explore** the world was I then able to take in so much more and give so much back.

• The only way I was able to peacefully enter a school building again was because I felt safe. I felt this sense of security because my director gave me a hug. Through her **Touch**, she told my nervous system I was going to be okay.

I've learned that I can't control what happens in my life, but I can control my reactions. I've chosen to look at my anxiety as a blessing. Though I've faced a whole lot of pain at such young age, without it I wouldn't be helping teenagers with the ASSET model.

The struggles I went through are being used to help others, and that's the blessing that was hidden in my anxiety.

About the Author

Tessa Zimmerman was a seventeen-year-old senior at Easton Country Day School in Easton, Connecticut at this writing. Her life's passion is to use her own experience to help teenagers and the world, using her ASSET model, an approach designed to help teenagers become masters of themselves through empowerment. She founded the ASSET Foundation so she could share her wisdom with the world. Her website, IAmTessa.com, presents the ASSET method in articles that are relatable to teens. Tessa has been a contributor to FTNS radio, and had a segment called, "Tessa Tries It Out." Tessa strongly believes that teenagers have the power to change our world for the better, if they're first given a chance to overcome their own personal obstacles.

Part Three

Learning from Loss

Just a Bump in the Road

Cynthia Anderson

There I was at a Denver Hospital, far from home, in the free program for poor unwed mothers, my legs in stirrups, ready to have my baby. But I was not going to welcome this baby. I was going to say goodbye.

As if I didn't feel terrible enough, the way I was being treated was cruel. I felt used by the medical students and residents, seen only as a body to be practiced on. *Just because I have no money or a husband doesn't mean I'm stupid or should be used as a guinea pig,* I was thinking.

My anger had been growing steadily, along with my baby, but when it came right down to it, I was really only angry at myself for getting into such a situation.

That's when the revelation came to me, right on the delivery table: I was going to be a midwife, one who never treats others the way I was being treated. I was never going to judge new mothers who have no money or status, but instead I would help other women through the most amazing transformation of all—pregnancy and the birth of their babies, no matter what circumstances they found themselves in.

My heart stayed in that nursery

A day later I was wheeled out of the hospital, my heart wrenched out of me, remaining there with my baby. You might be wondering right about now, thinking maybe that I had had a choice after all, that I really didn't *have to* leave him there. But at that troubled time in my life I honestly believed that was the best thing I could do for the little son I named Nathaniel, which means gift from God. He would be going to two parents who were able to plan and care for him as I believed I could not. I thought leaving him was the most responsible decision I could make.

It took many years before I learned that at those crucial moments in life it's far more important to listen to your heart than to your head. A social worker once gave me some advice that I've turned to many times over the years: "Never look back and second-guess your decision. You made the best decision you could make at that time."

My dad, who drove me out to Colorado when I was pregnant, and who certainly didn't condone the mess I had gotten myself into, was more colloquial about it. He said, with tears in his eyes for me, "Honey, this is just a bump in the road."

These words have carried me to this day.

Depression rarely left me over the next couple of months, and even years. At first I didn't want to eat. I slept all the time and cried the rest of the time, with no interest in other people or doing much of anything.

Then I started to come to life. Does time really heal all wounds? Was it time talking to me now, or was it my higher wisdom who gave me the idea to become a midwife while I was still on the delivery table? More likely it was a combination, along with my determination not to give in to the lethargy of depression, the determination to listen to a little voice inside me, spurring me on, telling me to move forward, to become a midwife so I could be there for other women in a powerful way.

Another way of seeing depression

Four years later I was finishing up nursing school, with a double major of social work and nursing, fast-tracked into the midwifery school, finding out first-hand that there's nothing better to take your mind off your pain than staying busy.

Still, my mood swings tended to leave me in the dumps, with thoughts of suicide plaguing me at times. I credit Bill, a good friend of mine, for teaching me one of my life's most precious lessons when he told me that I had a choice to be depressed or not. That did the trick. From that day on I have been able to get myself out of a depressed state simply by choosing to be happy. Sound too simple? But it really can be.

Brain chemistry is triggered by what we think about, so in effect *we become our thoughts.* I didn't get a chance to thank Bill, but I'm thanking him now. It's amazing to me how we touch each other with our words and wisdom, often not even knowing what we have given others. I know I have to credit myself as well, however, for being open to receiving that wisdom.

When I turned thirty, I celebrated with a Red Stripe beer on the black volcanic sand beach at Santa Lucia's Anse Chastanet resort, which cost over $300 a night. That price was for all the other people, as I paid a mere $11 a night, since the owners let the volunteers from the Catholic Mission Hospital have a break. I was finally a midwife, working with St.

Lucian women, catching their babies in the middle of the night, playing at the beach during the day. No bumps in the road, just smooth, easy riding as I sailed the Caribbean to St. Martinique with other doctors, nurses and midwives, vacationed on Barbados, learned to dance reggae, and made rum punch.

I was learning to trust my skills as a midwife, and even had a New Year's Eve baby named after me. Life here was easier, slower, and kinder, even for the babies, who received a daily coconut oil massage from their midwife. This really was a good life.

Making money has not always been top priority for me, but getting paid a dollar a day—literally—is a strain on the finances, so after six glorious months I was back home, working as a labor and delivery nurse at a teaching hospital. All nurses know that July is the scary time in the hospital, when the new residents arrive.

Face-to-face with an appalling memory

During my first July at the hospital I was confronted with my painful past when a new resident asked me to let him know when an eighteen-year-old woman in labor was getting ready to push, because he was planning to use forceps on her *for practice*. This procedure requires cutting the woman, so that the forceps fit inside. It can irreparably harm the baby, especially if the doctor is not skilled. I was beyond appalled and made sure the resident was not notified until the baby's head was crowning, which would be much too late to use forceps.

As if that were not enough, when I complained to

my supervisor about the resident I was told I should have given the resident that experience!

That job did not last long.

Later I worked as a midwife for about a year, then left my job, sold my belongings, put everything into a small car, and moved up to Canada to be with the man I loved. We had been dating for four years and I was ready for forever.

Forever didn't last long. Only two weeks later, with a broken spirit and heart, I headed back home after the love of my life told me he didn't love me any more.

Talk about bumps in the road! This one seemed insurmountable. But we never know what is around life's next bend. It's often a better beginning, and so it was for me when I found myself, three months later, halfway around the world, in charge of the Midwifery Obstetrics Ward in a Thai refugee camp. That area was—affectionately or not—known as "the armpit," but it offered me opportunities to travel and learn about life and another culture. The bumps in the road there were *literally* bumps in the road. I know this experience was partly about running away from my problems, but this was a perfect place to grieve my loss, as the Cambodians had lost so much more than I had, and that kind of perspective is sometimes all one needs.

Birthing babies in a war zone

At night we were required to leave, to go back to our safe compound while the camp became a war zone. One night I got special permission to stay in order to be in attendance while my lead midwife gave birth. I did, and was privy to all the local rituals I hadn't seen before, such as the tradition of washing the baby in Singha beer after it's born!

The camp of 211,000 eventually emptied out under our guidance. After thirteen years of camp life, everyone was going home. The oldest feared what they would find at home, having lived the horrors of the Khmer Rouge made famous by the movie, *The Killing Fields*. Because the youngest had known nothing but life in the camp, they thought water and food came from trucks instead of fields.

I went home as well, taking with me the unmentionable war stories I had been trusted with, but I also left knowing that out of the deepest despair can come hope and renewal. The lotus flower blooms from the mud.

I then went from a refugee camp to a summer camp, where, as camp nurse, I took care of bumps and bruised campers instead of worrying about malaria and cholera. My job opportunities included becoming a foster mom to ten-year-old identical twin boys, the same age as my Nathaniel. I couldn't have been happier or loved them more fiercely if they had been my own. It was as if I had been given another chance to be a mom.

Three months later their father came back into their lives, taking them from me. This time it was not my choice to give up a child. Was this Karma? All the pain of saying goodbye to Nathan came back tenfold.

I no longer wanted to go on with life, with its endless, unbearable bumps, ruts, holes. Yet I knew from the past there was going to be another bend, and around it things would be better. My job was just to wait, and meanwhile to work at turning my attitude to positive. I picked up running (literally, this time), which helped increase my positive brain endorphins.

Filling in my missing pieces

Then I met the man I was destined for. This felt like a new beginning, a welcome relief from the pain and loss. This was a man full of spirituality, talent, and love. An artist in all ways. Where one of us was lacking, the other had that piece, so together we were complete. My soul had found its mate. We moved together through the next part of our journey, reaching new heights and depths.

I had been working as a nurse and midwife for a long time, and as time passed I realize there was a missing ingredient in my practice. A seed that my dad had planted in my being had been growing for a long time. He had doctored himself with natural medicine, curing his gout and high blood pressure with nutrition and herbs. *Organic Gardening* and *Prevention* magazines were part of my growing up. I knew the medicine I had always gravitated to was this natural medicine, from the earth and from the heart.

This holism of mind, body, and spirit was what was missing in my practice.

I went back to school to become a doctor of this medicine, where the goal is to get to the underlying cause of disease instead of covering it up, so that the body, mind, and spirit are allowed to heal.

I started Naturopathic school and got married, both at age forty-one. Oh yes, my dad was able to recite his "Honey, it's just a bump in the road" speech several more times during the following years, till we all celebrated my graduation, four years later.

My work as a Naturopathic doctor was fulfilling, but I still ached for something else. My spirit was unfolding. I was introduced to the concept of energetic attraction and attended an amazing course called Avatar, which I consider the "naturopathic medicine" of therapy, since it concentrates on uncovering the underlying cause of mental anguish, instead of covering it up. During the first course, I was broken wide open as I reached the core of the experience of leaving Nathaniel.

Healed from the inside out, I was now able to move forward more fully in my life. Part of the Avatar process was to put our goals out to the universe. I wrote down my intention to have a television show in order to tell others about Naturopathic medicine. The Universe answered, and *poof*, three weeks later I was the host of my very own radio show.

I was home! Nothing had ever felt more right in my life as I sat there with my headphones firmly in place, in front of the microphone, sharing the possibilities of healing with natural medicine. My dad was my weekly guest, known as Pop Anderson, "The Backwoods Gardener."

Dad, who referred to me as his doctor, expressed his worry and concern one day, when he called me up to discuss his recent fatigue, as well as symptoms that included lumps under his skin that were growing. Somewhere in my gut I knew it was cancer, but how could my dad, my mentor, the natural man of medicine have cancer?

Over the course of several months Dad's fatigue deepened. He wrote on his Christmas card that year, "Thanks for setting up my appointment with the Naturopathic doctor [an ND closer to where Dad lived], maybe we will get to the bottom of this."

I got the call soon after—my dad was having a heart attack and being flown to a heart hospital. Ironically, I was on my way to do a radio show about heart health, and through sheer willpower I did the show, hoping it would help some listener who was tuning in.

I got the first possible flight down in order to be with my Pop, and was told that when they opened him up they found cancer. He was in the ICU when I saw him, full of tubes and IVs. The nurse was keeping him sedated, since every time he woke up he tried to pull out his breathing tube. I stayed with him all night. He was crying a good deal and kept trying to say something. Later, when the tube came out, he blurted, "I can't talk." I believe this was a premonition of things to come.

Between us girls and Mom, someone was always at his side, as things went from bad to worse. My dad, who at eighty-two was still able to do 900 jumps on the trampoline, was told he had clogged arteries, diabetes, and cancer. I sat with him as he shook his head. Pointing to his heart, he said, "Honey, I can deal with this." And then, indicating his thymus, where he had been told his cancer was, he said "But I don't know about this." My sister was with him when the nurse, following the doctor's orders, gave him too much insulin, putting him in a coma.

Finally, we were complete
Shortly after waking up from that, Dad had a stroke, after which he, who had exemplified the word "articulate," could no longer talk to us. One of my brothers rushed down to help us make sense of it all, and as a team we were finally able to convince the doctor to let us take Dad home.

Dad was visibly relieved to be home, but kept pointing at the four of us, counting 1, 2, 3, 4 and shrugging his shoulders. Finally my missing brother joined us, which got a "WOW" from Dad. We were complete, all five kids and his wife of fifty-three years. Out of his pain, Dad gave us the bittersweet gift of sharing this time with him. The closeness this experience gave us is beyond words. Suffice it to say that old wounds were healed and new bonds made between all of us.

I had a hard time letting go, trying with all my homeopathics to cure, heal, and save my father.

Nothing worked, and nine days later he was dead.

This particular bump in the road led me into a brick wall full of glass. I vacillated between numbness and pulling out the glass to let the blood flow. There was no middle road. I had been my dad's doctor, after all. I was supposed to save him, and I didn't. With the help of others and the wise words "Physician, heal thyself," I realized I never had control over him or anyone else. My dad was his own doctor; I was there only because he allowed me into his inner sanctum for a consult. He lived the way he wanted, and in the end died that way, surrounded by loved ones in a beautiful creation called hospice, where all the workers are angels as they help guide others through dying, every day.

As I heal, my road is still full of deep divots. Some catch my breath and stop me in my tracks, but I take time to listen and to learn the lessons waiting for me. Grief and loss intermingle with Dad's words: "Remember to always celebrate life."

Younger women who are looking for a cross between a mentor and a mother seem to find me. One called me today. She was in pain, and needed help. She had just found out she was pregnant, but didn't have a job. She knew she didn't want to "get rid of it," which was what her friends were telling her was the smart thing to do. I gave her some words of advice: "Honey, listen to your heart and know this is just a bump in the road."

We all have our own journeys, but if we travel with an open heart and positive attitude, keeping the focus on others instead of ourselves, life can be remarkable.

About the Author

Dr. Cynthia Anderson, RN, CNM, ND brings to her practice over twenty-five years experience as a Nurse and Midwife in the United States as well as in Thailand, Cambodia, and St. Lucia. She has been treating body, mind and spirit as a Naturopathic Doctor since 2005, always seeking to get to the underlying cause of a disease or condition. She is part of a holistic team at SabitaHolisticCenter. com. Certified in Wilson's Temperature Syndrome, she helps identify and treat sub-clinical hypothyroidism. Some of her other specialties are natural options for anxiety, weight management, and identifying and treating gluten sensitivity. Dr. Anderson is an adjunct Professor at the Naturopathic College of the University of Bridgeport, where she enjoys teaching gynecology and obstetrics. She recently returned to Denver to present at the National Midwifery convention on natural options for women during menopause. She lives in Connecticut and can be reached at DocCinMid@gmail.com.

My Great Gift of Grief

Sandra Champlain

June 23, 2010.

I was looking up at the blue sky and the perfect airplane formation above. As one plane pulled away from the others, tears ran down my face. It was the "Missing Man" formation, flown in honor of my dad, retired pilot John Champlain, who had died the month before. While there were hundreds of people standing around me at this memorial service for him, I felt so alone as I mourned the loss of my father.

I had no idea that three years later I would create something that would allow thousands of people around the world to heal and live greater lives.

Dad was diagnosed with cancer five months prior to his death. He had been a strong and athletic man—so strong, in fact, that at the age of seventy-four he would ride his bike twenty miles daily, just to keep fit. A pain in his back led him to the doctor, where he found out there was a tumor breaking apart his spine. The tumor was irradiated over the following months, but the damage had been done. He suffered such severe pain that a pain pump was attached directly to his body. Unfortunately, his blood tests continually indicated that cancer was growing somewhere in his body, yet the doctors could not find it to treat it.

I was the only single child at the time, and had relocated to Daytona Beach, Florida, to be by Dad's side. My siblings were all married with kids, so my being the one to help Dad seemed the obvious choice.

A dark place gets even darker

Because we have always been a reasonably close family, I never could have predicted what was to come. Over the months preceding Dad's death and the months that followed, severe arguments between my siblings and me became the norm. We would fight about what Dad said, what Dad wanted, and what care facilities he should go to. Even after his death, the accusations continued, and there was even fighting about his belongings and how to handle his affairs.

Somehow in the middle of all this I got labeled the greedy one. So not only did I lose my dad, but my relationships with my siblings came to an end.

Losing my dad, especially in that way, brought me the most severe emotional pain I have ever felt. I would cry so hard that I would buckle over, unable to even stand up.

I would wake up crying. I replayed the events before and after his death, over and over in my mind. At first I did not want to talk to anyone and kept to myself most of the time. Whenever I was willing to talk, I would find myself telling my story over and over again, repeating it to anyone who would listen.

I was in such a dark place. And it got darker: Not talking to my siblings meant I was no longer able to see their children. That *really* hurt.

I am not a person who has ever considered suicide, but that time was so horrible and painful that I became able to understand people who choose to end their lives. I couldn't see an end to my pain. How long would it take for my mind and body to come out of this awful place?

Suddenly, a chain of thoughts spoke to me, saying, "This is not me! I am not this person. What is wrong with me? Why can't I pull myself out of this? *I wonder, is this what grief is?*"

That moment was the turning point for me. I began to explore the world of grief. I rediscovered some familiar statements about grief and its five stages: denial, anger, bargaining, depression, and acceptance. Although I was grateful that there was an explanation as to why I was feeling the way I was, there was still a question I needed answered, "Is grief responsible for tearing apart my relationships with my brother and sisters?"

How grief remaps our brain's landscape

Those experiencing grief need an outlet. That's why mothers who lose children in accidents often become involved with organizations set up to stop people from drinking or texting while driving. Eric Clapton wrote a powerful song after the death of his child and poured his emotions into it. I, Sandra Champlain, responded by giving my all to researching the world of grief.

My research produced extraordinary results. I uncovered the fact that our brains actually go through a state of shock when we grieve. Our brains have to rewire themselves to function in the new reality we are facing. The more we love what we've lost, the harder we grieve, whether the source is the death of a loved one, or the breakup of a relationship, or a change in our health, job, or financial situation.

We have a feel-good neurotransmitter in our brains called serotonin. When we grieve, the serotonin level sharply drops, and anger and depression take over. However, what was important for me to realize was that serotonin also has an impact on the memory, perception, and communication centers of our brains. So grieving people cannot clearly focus on the world happening around them, cannot store information correctly, and cannot communicate their thoughts properly.

This phenomenon quickly left the realm of theory as I began to recognize its disturbing influence in my life. An example of this would be a conversation I had with my sister about my father's care. I spoke my thoughts as clearly as possible, knowing that she would repeat everything to my siblings. Three times I repeated my words to my sister and each time she turned my message into other words. I grew frustrated. Only by being patient was I able to get her to repeat to me exactly what I had told her. However, when she went to repeat my words to my siblings, she once again distorted my message, making them more upset with me than before.

Looking back, I realize that my sister's grieving brain could not handle the information that was coming in, so of course she wasn't easily able to repeat it back to me. For all I know, *my* grieving brain was telling her the story differently when I spoke each time, as well! There is no way to know for sure what happened. Was it my fault? Was it my sister's?

No. It was grief's fault.

The more I investigated, the more I learned. Almost fifty percent of siblings come apart when a parent dies—a staggering figure. Eighty percent of couples get divorced if a child dies, and ninety percent get divorced if one of the two gets diagnosed with a life-threatening illness. One million people a year commit suicide due to grief and depression.

Why?

Grief impacts us in ways we cannot imagine and are not educated about, especially since the world rarely talks about grief. With this knowledge I set out to share what I found in the hope of preventing further destruction from grief. I recorded an audio called, "How to Survive Grief," and posted it on the Internet. Just a few posts to friends on Facebook rapidly turned into several thousand people listening, with fifteen countries around the world downloading it. Doctors began recommending the audio, and so did suicide prevention agencies. I began to receive emails from people, telling me how my words had saved their relationships, eased their pain, and prevented suicides. The pain I speak of in that audio is very common to many.

"It was grief, it wasn't me."
I had given one friend a freshly burned copy of my audio on a CD. His wife had left him for another man, and I told him, "Grief is grief, this may or may not help you, but take it." Several months later he came to visit me. His words are what made me realize I had to write a book. He said, "Sandra, I was so depressed when you gave me that CD. I literally had already planned my suicide. But when I listened to it, it was as if you were speaking directly to me. You knew exactly what was in my head and what I was thinking. That's when I realized I was experiencing grief and there was nothing wrong with me. I followed your suggestions, and not only am I happy, but I fell in love. I wouldn't be on the planet without you, Sandra. Thank you."

Somehow, some way, my simply declaring to myself that I was going to write a book started opening doors. I found myself talking to many people about what I wanted to do, and eventually my friends introduced me to their friends, who introduced me to their friends! I took a risk and attended a course called Author 101 University, where I met publishers, agents, and other people with dreams of sharing what was in their hearts. I found myself telling my familiar story about Dad and my new knowledge about grief. However, every book needs a "hook," a title to pull readers in and motivate them to buy. I had such a hook, but was scared to death to tell anyone.

You see, I am not just someone who has investigated grief. I have spent the better part of fifteen years studying the controversial subject of "life after death." A fear of death led me to discovering the undeniable proof I needed: that we don't die. I have seen the words "We Don't Die" in my head for years, knowing that some day I would write a book with that title.

During that entire weekend at Author 101 University I spoke only about my grief research, too afraid to tell people about my other research until, just after the class ended, when David Hancock, the founder of Morgan James Publishing, asked me why I had attended the conference. I sat face-to-face with him as he held my hands, knowing how scared I was to tell him my story. I told him about Dad, my siblings, the grief, the audio that has helped thousands, and my journey to learning about life after death. "Who am I to write a book like this?" I asked him. His eyes filled with tears and he simply responded, "Who are you not to?"

I will not tell you that the journey to becoming a published author was easy, but when someone believes in you, things can happen fast. I followed his instructions and submitted a book proposal, including who I am, why the message is important, a few sample chapters, and so much more. It took over a month to get an answer, but when I did, I got a "Yes, we'd love to publish your book, Sandra."

That was only eighteen months ago, and in that time my life has gone from pain to fame! In the five short months that the book has been for sale, over one thousand copies have sold. It has become a #1 international bestseller and currently sits in bookstores next to Dr. Phil, Stephen Covey, and Anthony Robbins. Not just a book on grief, or life after death, it is a book on living life fully. I like to call it a handbook for living. I start my radio and television media tours very soon, and my publisher says that by the end of the year I will be telling my story on "Good Morning America" and on "Ellen, the Ellen DeGeneres Show." Wow.

Life is rarely easy for any of us. I have not met one person who has had smooth sailing. There are ups and downs and sometimes more downs—and then still more downs. I personally believe that you and I are here to live our lives fully, to learn and to grow, just like a seed planted in the cold, dark earth that has to search for moisture, fight its way to the surface, and never know why, till one day it breaks through the surface into daylight. The journey might not be easy, since it begins with the seed struggling to survive the temperature, the wind and the rain. But one day a flower blooms. It may not be able to see itself and recognize that it is a flower, but it can bring a huge amount of comfort and happiness to another.

Wherever you are in your journey, you can rest assured that, although you may not see the path, and you may not understand your journey, you are just where you need to be to one day comfort someone else. Life may not always go the way you intend, but if you trust, you will see that you've had to endure a lot to be the magnificent person you are now.

Yes, I am talking to you, and yes, you are magnificent.

About the Author

Sandra Champlain is the author of the #1 international best-selling book *We Don't Die - A Skeptic's Discovery of Life After Death* and the CDs *How to Survive Grief* and *The Law of Chocolate*. She owns The Kent Coffee and Chocolate Company in Kent, Connecticut, and travels with world-class racecar teams, providing hospitality for the United SportsCar Racing series. A sought-after speaker, author, and entrepreneur, Sandra is committed to making a difference in the lives of others. For more information, please visit SandraChamplain.com.

It's About the Shoes

Mel Morgan

It's funny how things—and your life—can change in an instant.

Four days prior to my twenty-fifth birthday, my roommates and I were watching *Kindergarten Cop*, with Arnold Schwarzenegger. We were joking around because Arnold's character says he has a headache and one of the children says, "It's a tumor." Arnold replies, "I do not have a tumor." My roommates and I laughed about it because I was going to the doctor in the morning for my test results.

Not so funny the next morning.

Frankly, when the doctor told me it was a tumor, I do not even remember how I responded, how I got into the car or back into my apartment. I do remember my roommate finding me sitting in a corner in our living room. The next couple of weeks would be a blur, with more tests, blood tests, X-rays, MRIs, CAT scans and a second opinion at Sloan-Kettering—only to find that the doctors best suited to treating me were the ones I was already seeing.

Finally I was diagnosed with a sarcoma in my ankle, stage II cancer. We began chemotherapy right away.

The hardest thing about getting cancer was telling my parents. I felt I was hurting them, when what I really wanted was to protect them. My brother sang me a song that helped to comfort me, which to this day has such special meaning to me. It's Bob Marley's "Three Little Birds" song. Some of the lyrics are, "Don't worry about a thing/cause every little thing gonna be all right." Those words gave me hope. My family is very supportive and provided a place for me to turn to for strength. They also did not "baby" me, but treated me with love and kindness. I love the way my dad would rub my head after I had lost all my hair, as if I were a genie and he could make a wish.

The best remedies, not the easiest
Fast forward. Three months of chemo, and the tumor did not shrink. Noticing that the tumor was not shrinking, they said the best remedies would be to continue chemo and amputation. My oncology doctor was so compassionate and explained everything to me: how we would progress with the chemo, what I needed to do, and ways in which I would be able to live. I am thankful for my oncologist, as well as for my other doctors throughout my illness. His great attitude, his listening to me when I thought every ache and pain meant I had some other illness, his assurances, all meant so much to me.

The next course of action was to remove my leg below the knee. That was the hardest decision I had to make. In college I ran, played tennis, and walked a lot, so of course I wondered how this would affect my life Also, I was a shoe ADDICT! I loved shoes—patent leather, boots, you name it.

How is a young girl with a shoe addiction going to deal with losing her leg? I would soon find out. I also had other concerns. I am a young single woman. How is this going to affect my dating life? Who is going to date a girl like me?

I had a below-the-knee amputation. I remember being in the back of the car with my parents on the way to the hospital and saying good-bye to my foot. I thanked it for all that it had done for me. I was thankful that I had it for the number of years I had. I looked at my toes, I looked at the lines in my foot, and I looked at my ankle—swollen and purple, and wondered why it betrayed me. It was time to let go.

I woke up at the hospital, not really feeling much different. I was surrounded by friends and family and I was so happy—I think that was the morphine (ha!). One of my brothers stayed the night with me in my hospital room and I was so grateful. It helped me to not be afraid the first night. He took me to all of my appointments, to chemo, and made me laugh with me when I felt awful.

Next I had to learn how to walk. After receiving my first prosthesis I was happy to be mobile again. Music played such an important part in my recovery. I would play "Coming Out of the Dark" by Gloria Estefan over and over. She had been in a bad bus accident and she regained her mobility and remained strong.

Who would think that your arms play a part in your walking? I sure didn't. On TV I had seen people walking between what appeared to be the kind of parallel bars that gymnasts used, and I didn't quite understand how that worked. Well, now I do. Those bars are paramount, as they enabled me to have support for each step I took. Each step felt so wonderful.

I walked like a robot until I learned how to use my arms properly, and how arm movement is an important function with my gait. It was painful at times, and I was really scared that I would fall over and hurt myself.

Baby steps with the best of brothers

I learned to take one step at a time and to have hope. Baby steps. I also learned that even though I fell down, I could get back up again. It wasn't as easy as when I had both legs, but it was manageable. I just had to take my time, figure it out, and get up. My family and my faith allowed me to have hope. It helped to have brothers who were into sports. They were positive and upbeat, telling me that it's all possible and that I just needed to persevere, that I can do whatever I put my mind to.

People can also be jerks. A year or so after the surgery, I went to a bar with my friends and some guy called me "Peg." I innocently said, "That's not my name," and he said, "Yes it is. Peg... peg leg, get it?" I cried and walked home. My friend Ron said to me, "That guy was a jerk, and remember that you are alive and well." Thanks Ron—you are a good egg!

My nephew had an awesome take on my limb loss and my prosthetic. I went to visit my family and my nephew was playing basketball with one of his friends. He said to them, "Come and meet my aunt, she is a like a transformer." Leave it to a child to put it all into perspective. He was not afraid of me, instead he saw me as robot-like, with certain powers.

In the spring, I finished my course of chemo. At around that time, one of my friends would often pick me up and take me on drives to look at Dogwood trees. We would just laugh and laugh. She even taught me how to drive again. Brake, *Brake!* She said it would feel good to have my freedom again, to go where I wanted to go, whenever I wanted to go. And she was right.

Hello shoe world, I'm back!

Years later, I moved to Chicago for work and was fortunate enough to go to the Rehabilitation Institute of Chicago (RIC). My eyes were opened there, as I met other amputees and joined a support group. It was there that I saw a woman, a double amputee, wearing the cutest shoes. I felt so joyous to see her in cute shoes. Hello shoe world, I am back! You see, up until then I had been wearing shoes that tie, not so fashionable. One day I wore ballet slippers and tripped at work. The shoe flew off into the planter box and the person walking behind me and I laughed and laughed. I guess that's why my prosthetist told me to wear tie shoes. Safety was not my first priority, looking cute and stylish was.

Anyway, on to the Rehab Institute of Chicago—what an amazing place! I had a wonderful doctor. Now he is the director of the Institute and has developed the first bionic arm—go figure. I tell you, I feel so blessed to know that I have had some of the best doctors and medical care. I am so grateful because, had I lost my leg many, many years ago or lived in a different country, I would not have had the opportunities to progress the way I have.

I have met some of the most wonderful people who have proven that missing a limb does not mean that you are not whole. It just means you are missing a limb.

I have met a Paralympic skier and was just astounded by what she accomplished as an above-the-knee amputee. I have met a woman missing an arm who amazed me as she commuted into the City each and every day through the hustle and bustle. *How does she carry her handbag and hold on while standing on the train?* I wondered.

I find I have more compassion toward others now, because you see each of us has a story, and in its own way, each is a story of triumph, overcoming odds and becoming a champion. We are all warriors. It's within each and every one of us. Sometimes you have to dig deep to find it, sometimes you don't, but it is there. We are all overcomers.

I have lots of shoes. Sure, they are flats, but they are stylish. I feel girly and hope to someday be able to have a high-heeled leg, a swim leg, and my everyday leg. Do you know they make prosthetic legs with split toes? Hairs on the leg? Flexible ankles? Believe me, there are many different types of legs out there and many different shades of colors. I am thankful for my prosthetic leg as well as my sound leg. I am thankful to be mobile. I can go places, I can drive, and I can get around. There is a famous female amputee by the name of Aimee Mullins and she is fierce!!! Great attitude, and she has been a shoe model who brags about her twelve different pairs of legs. An amputee who models shoes… Gotta love her! By the way, she's also an athlete who holds world records.

Amputees are doing great things. Skiing, running—it's all possible. As for the dating, I have dated. My leg is not an issue to the right kind of guy. The great thing is that a prosthetic leg is a good barometer for meeting someone. If he has an issue with it, he's just not the right person for me.

Anything is possible, if you put your mind to it. "As a man thinketh, so he shall be."

Think good thoughts, *think that you can and you will.* Be grateful for the little things, and know that you are not alone. That's what I do. Sure, I get frustrated at times, but that just means I need to stop, have some alone time and get back out there.

I hope to run again someday. I know it's possible!

About the Author

Mel Morgan is the pen name of an East Coast resident who wishes to remain anonymous.

Missing

Betty Ruddy

It was autumn, a time of change. I yearned for something predictable. I tried to check in on Jack and Samantha at least once each day. How was their day at the office? What was new in their love lives? How were their associates: Vivian, Danny, Martin, and Elena? These "friends" of mine, FBI-agent characters on the television series *Without a Trace,* were oblivious to the interest I took in their trials and tribulations. But when I skipped a day of touching base with them, I was bereft. There was something about those energetic agents earnestly searching for missing persons that I—a lost woman myself—was drawn to.

I had just separated from my husband after thirty-two years. It's a long story—they usually are—full of many satisfactions, but also loneliness, disappointments, and unsuccessful fresh starts. I told my husband it was a trial separation. He filed for divorce. My sister- in-law stopped speaking to me. My young adult children were confused, angry, trying hard to be fair and grown up about it all.

I signed a month-to-month lease on a fully furnished apartment in one of those half-suburban/half-urban satellite cities that sprout near larger, older ones. It was a city of cars; no one walked unless it was just down the block. Nearby upscale malls brightly boasted of the city's prosperity. I had picked my apartment building in part because of its security features and in part because it was across the street from a two-story regional library branch.

I had not lived alone in thirty-three years. Before that, rarely had I done so happily. Still, I thought the independence and privacy of the apartment was what

I craved, and for the first two days I could scarcely believe my luck. I could do whatever I wanted: read and write, explore my new neighborhood, lose track of time in the library stacks. I lived from one moment to the next without giving a thought to what someone else needed or wanted.

What I hadn't counted on was the silence. Despite the buses braking below my window twenty-four hours a day, the air around me was eerily hushed. I longed for the voice in my head that reminded me that other people occupied the same space I did, even if they weren't home, that other people needed me, if only to be around. I had brought with me from home a few clothes, a few books, two small bookcases, and a knick-knack or two. They didn't make me feel at home.

This new quiet might have propelled me out into the world to shop, eat, go to a movie, see friends. Instead, it paralyzed me. I ate what I wanted when I wanted, but only if I could get myself to drive eight blocks to the grocery store. I could stay up late and sleep in late—that is, if I could sleep at all. Books were once a source of solace and pleasure, but I couldn't summon the concentration reading requires. One day, I went to the library and felt as if I had entered a foreign country, one where I had once known the customs, liked the food. I stayed for ten minutes and never returned.

The evenings loomed like chasms. Although I had not been a frequent television watcher, the large set in the living room was a siren whose song entranced me every night. Then one day I turned on the set, hoping to catch *Law and Order* reruns on TNT, and happened upon a rerun of *Without a Trace*. FBI agents were searching for a prison inmate who disappeared shortly before his scheduled release date. Like all the other episodes I watched during those months, the agents worked hard to follow the missing person's trail. When asked why he was so dedicated, Jack, the boss, answered, "My job is to find people who are missing." I know it's sappy, but there were times I wanted to think he meant finding me.

The television set may have enabled me to record shows, but I was too disoriented to try, so I watched the first runs and reruns when they were shown. It came to be that the only time that meant anything to me was television time. The rest of the world had all but disappeared. Or maybe, no longer tethered to a familiar place, a well-rehearsed role, I was the one who had disappeared. And no one was looking for me.

I was experiencing my life in fragments. My ideas of what might happen in the future floated through my brain, sometimes thrilling, sometimes frightening. They seemed disconnected from reality. I lived only in the next moment, as if my mind had shut down rather than make some decision about the future. Memories or anticipations no longer provided companionship, only the guilt I felt about my husband, my children—even my mother, over a year dead. I worried about what would happen, should the marriage end, and what would happen if it didn't. I was no longer the woman I knew as myself: good mother, loving wife, strong, steadfast woman. I was discovering parts of myself I had always known were there but I had never wanted to face. Somehow I had to fit these missing pieces of me into a new narrative.

Somewhere along the way I had lost the ability to suspend disbelief, and had to acknowledge that I had been lonely for a long time and had hid that loneliness from my husband and myself. Jim and I had started our relationship with enthusiasm, but weren't prepared to deal with our differences. He was circumspect, which I took for detachment and I was insecure, which he took for being demanding.

My decision to separate could be undone, but as much as I tried to talk myself into it, I couldn't do it. And yet, neither was I ready to follow the voice that said: "GO." After a while, the two sides of me had nothing new to say, no matter how much they chattered, and eventually the thoughts spun in such tight spirals that they formed one large knot of such desperation and indecision that I began to think any story, no matter how jumbled, would do.

Does anyone remember *Barney Miller*, the late 1970s television series about a New York police precinct populated with a cast of offbeat police officers? One episode sticks in my mind. The station house is visited by a sweet old lady who tells of terrible fights in the apartment across the airshaft and of a young woman who, after one rather disturbing argument a couple of days earlier, was never seen again. As I remember, it takes most of the thirty-minute episode for the kindly officers to realize that the woman—in her terrible loneliness—was confusing her favorite soap opera with the drama of real life.

On many nights during the three months I lived in that furnished apartment, I worried that I was more like that woman than I would ever want to admit. How easy, I realized, to go from being a sane wife and mother to a mentally unbalanced single older woman. I suffered blinding flashes of fear. Once I woke from a dream in which a strange man had found his way to my bedroom doorway, me unprotected despite having checked and double-checked the locks on all the windows and doors. Mostly I wondered: What did other single women think about? Were they afraid of their aloneness? Were their thoughts, like mine, nothing but a pile of wood shavings? What did they tell themselves about their lives? Did they watch a lot of television?

As I went through my day—on a good day doing errands, emailing, talking on the phone, on a bad day doing Sudoku puzzles non-stop for hours—I felt my day building toward "my program," hoping the episodes available that night were, ideally, ones I had not seen, or, acceptably, ones I had seen only once before. I usually took my fix with dinner, sitting on the couch, as if I had company. Almost always, the missing people are found. Almost always they hadn't known the FBI was looking for them. Almost always—no matter why they were missing—they are glad to be found.

I slowly gained energy, and one day a shift took place inside me. I realized that I was more willing to take a chance on what might lie ahead than return to what I had. To leave the marriage would be to leave behind big chunks of myself. But I couldn't bring myself to forgo what seemed like a life full of new experiences. I finally found my way out of that bland apartment and sterile neighborhood and moved to New York City. My two adult children lived there, as did a few friends. I signed a year's lease on a two-bedroom apartment and moved my stuff from storage in Seattle. I did not adjust well to New York. I was excited about being there, but everything I had to or wanted to do seemed a huge undertaking. A scent of failure dogged my every step. It clung to my clothes and wasn't sure I would ever be able to wash it out. I wasn't sure I deserved to.

A month later I went to Florida to pack up my things from our second home, which my husband was keeping. I was taking four pieces of Danish Modern furniture from the 1950s, handed down from old friends of my parents. I was taking my custom-made beach bag and my collection of sharks' teeth. I was taking my great aunt's green and gold sewing basket and the black lacquered cigarette box my uncle had brought back from his tour of duty in the Philippines for my parents' wedding gift. My sister-in-law was helping me, and we good-naturedly haggled over one item: a charcoal portrait of my father done by his college roommate, which my mother had always had hanging in her bedroom. After I promised I would send it to her and my brother in a few months, Cathy gave way.

Three days after my return to New York, I realized I had not received the promised call from the moving company, giving me some idea when my things would begin their journey northward. My call to the movers was answered promptly by Carol, the nice young woman I had been dealing with. "I'll have someone call you back about that," she said.

Five minutes later the phone rang. "This is Mr. _____ from Bekins Moving and Storage in Indiana," came a strong male voice. "We've been trying to reach you. I'm sorry to have to report that the truck on which your things were placed last Tuesday was stolen from the moving company lot, driven to North Port and set on fire. All the contents were burned to a crisp."

It took a couple of years for the shock of that loss to wear down to an occasional memory. Even now I sometimes think of the things on that truck, as well as things that were lost in other post-divorce moves. At first I felt I was being punished for creating such upheaval in my family. Then I felt guilty, as if I had been selfish for insisting on having those things. Finally, I mourned the loss of those things as a way of mourning all else that I had lost.

A lot of decisions I made in my life were calculated to avoid being alone, for fear of loneliness. Decisions about where to live, whom to marry. The irony is that they were so counterproductive. They kept me from being myself, from making decisions based in reality. And I ended up, at age sixty-four, alone after all.

I have lived by myself for two years now. I still look back sometimes with a little regret about the marriage. Still, I have come a long way from the paralysis of those days in that apartment. I am finding joy in the solitude and independence I looked for but couldn't find there. I have learned that you can't go through life trying to avoid loss; some kind of loss is unavoidable.

I have seen every *Without a Trace* episode at least twice. And, although the adventures of the FBI agents looking for missing persons helped keep me from going crazy, it turned out that I was the one who finally found myself.

About the Author

Betty Ruddy's work has been published in, among other places, *Fourth Genre* and *The Journal*. Two of her pieces were named Notable Essays by *Best American Essays*. She lives and writes in Kent, Connecticut, and owns an art and design store: BluArchCollection.com. She received her MFA from the Bennington College Writing Seminars in 2006.

Part Four

Mastership of Mind

Twelve Cents and
Ten Dreams

Joe Cirulli

I can still remember the moment. It was March of 1978 when the owner of the health club I managed sat me down to tell me about a few challenging issues he was facing. The first was his health. The second was his divorce.

And the third was that he was going bankrupt and the health club was going with him.

Did it scare me that my only source of livelihood and the only job I truly loved was ending? *Not in the least.*

My fearlessness was not because this was my first encounter with a health club going bankrupt. It was actually my *sixth.* I had been preparing for this moment long before I ever walked into this particular club.

I had never even planned on getting into this line of work for a living. In October of 1973 I came down to Gainesville, Florida from Upstate New York, simply to visit a friend. My plan was to stay for thirty days, then to return home to work and save some money. I still had two more years of college left. I did go home, only to return after Christmas, since the friend I was going to work with in construction thought it would be better for me to come back in April, after the winter weather broke. Mason work and snow didn't go together all that well.

Little did I know that the decision to return would not only set the course of my life, but would give me an opportunity to find out who I was.

The revealing upside-down view

I learned a long time ago that you really don't know a lot about the character of a person—even your own!—when everything is going well. The only way you'll find out is when everything in life is turned upside down. Sure enough, I was about to learn a great deal about myself.

I was fortunate to come from a good family, with parents who always stressed character and honesty. They did this in both their words and actions. My father was a Naval officer and my mother a nurse. Then there were my two older sisters, two younger sisters and two younger brothers. I guess any parents dealing with seven children had to have some exceptional qualities. Growing up in a middle-class family, I never really thought about success. I thought of working to make a living, but nothing much outside of that. I never had the mindset that I could accomplish great things, or even that I could determine the course of my life.

That changed one day when I found myself sitting in someone's office and opened a drawer. There sat a book called *The Power of Positive Thinking*, by Dr. Norman Vincent Peale. I wasn't much of a reader at the age of twenty, but for some reason I opened it and started reading about people who faced multiple challenges and overcame them, accomplishing extraordinary things simply by changing the way they thought, setting goals and meeting them.

I have a mind, I said to myself, *why can't I think like these people?*

So I immediately set some big goals.

This was the beginning of a whole new world for me, a world built on the inspiring stories of others who had accomplished extraordinary things while working through the worst of circumstances.

I've been asked many times how I could ever stick with an industry that was doomed to failure, and I could understand that thinking. But I never looked at it that way. I always felt that what our clubs did was vitally important to improving the health of so many people. It's just that what was missing was leadership that understood the *true* value of what we did, and not simply the financial reasons.

Down to twelve cents, and still not a "failure"
From the ages of nineteen to twenty-four, my life was simply about moving from one bankrupt health club to the next. I lived in closed-down clubs, in the clubs I was working in, and even in my car. During this time I remember getting down to my last twelve cents. *But the key is that I never saw myself as a failure.* Instead, I saw myself as someone building my internal résumé. You see, no matter what happened I found solace in books written by the people I would look at as my mentors, even if they were no longer alive or if I had never met them in person.

Their words resonated powerfully in my mind.

Once, when I was twenty-one, I found myself in a bookstore, looking for my next source of inspiration. One book in particular caught my attention. It's called *Think and Grow Rich*, by Napoleon Hill. I looked at it and thought *That's a cool title.* I

177

remember the description on the back: "This book has been responsible for more people becoming millionaires than any book ever written." Not that I ever thought about becoming a millionaire, especially after hitting the twelve-cent level, but it did get my attention.

So I brought it home and started to read. It said that in order to be successful, you have to know the secret. Secret! What secret? It couldn't be any simpler: You had to know what you wanted out of your life.

I pulled out a legal pad. I was ready.

I wrote a list with ten things on it:

• The first on the list was to own a health club in Gainesville, Florida. I had lived in two other cities, but Gainesville was for me.
• Second was to make health clubs respected in the Gainesville community. They had a terrible reputation because of all the bankruptcies.

Then I started to put some fun things down, like

• I'd have a home in the mountains, a home on the ocean and I'd build my parents a home.
• I'd make $100,000 dollars by the time I turned twenty-five.
• I'd own a little Mercedes, the kind the Six Million Dollar Man would drive in a TV show I used to watch as a kid.

- I'd become a black belt.
- I'd become a pilot and even own an airplane.
- I would travel all over America.
- I'd travel all over the world.
- I'd save a million dollars. Why a million? Because when I was growing up I'd always hear people say, "I wish I had a million dollars," so I figured I should put it on the list.

The next thing I knew to do was read my list. And I did, every night before I went to bed and every morning before work. I once heard a psychologist say, "You can't move away from what you're thinking, you're always moving in the direction of your dominant thoughts." He also said that there was value in reading your goals before your brain got filled with too many things.

So I read this list every day for years, including on the morning I was told the club was going bankrupt. Because I was able to look at the bankrupt health-club-owner's words as my opportunity to accomplish the first thing on my list, I surprised him by asking him if he would let me take over his bankrupt company and form a new one. I even told him I'd pay off his debts.

But the test is just beginning
Then it got even more interesting. The next day I received a letter from the landlord—actually a bank—that the health club was being evicted. I met with the

bank president, and he agreed to give me sixty days to raise the money so I could build a new club.

Though I didn't yet have the money sixty days later, I did find a building where I could relocate the club. I had an architect agree to design it, even after I told him I didn't have any money to pay him on the spot, assuring him I would some day.

I met with the bank president again, and persuasively encouraged him to give me thirty more days. Eventually, he gave in. One day before the new deadline I got a loan for $10,000, but since I had owed them $3300 from an earlier loan, I only received $6700.

That happened not a minute too soon, because that night the old landlord called to tell me the health club was closing the next day, and he wanted the key back. I told him I had some money—neglecting to mention how much—and set up an appointment with him for the next morning.

The next morning, my final day, I called the new landlord to tell him I was coming over to sign the lease, figuring that my having a lease in hand would convince the bank president to give me more time.

But what happened next stopped me in my tracks. He said he had just leased the space out to a national company, figuring it was a safer bet than a local company such as mine.

I was stunned. It was over, I thought.

I remember putting my head down on my desk, knowing I had been beaten. I left the health club and drove over to see a friend. As you can imagine, I was a slight wreck. I remember sitting across from him and telling him everything that happened during the previous ninety days. I told him about not getting the lease. I was in tears. I needed a hug or something, but no hug was coming from him. Instead he simply told me the truth: I had no choice—I had to find a new place. The only problem was that I felt there weren't many choices available. "Oh yeah," I told my friend, "and that's not all. I have to meet with the president of the bank today. He wants to shut me down."

Still no hug from my friend. But he had told me the truth.

For some reason, by the time I got to the bank president's office I wasn't upset anymore. I was actually *angry*. He said he wanted the key back. I told him I wasn't going to give him the key back. He said, "WHAT?" I said, "I'm not giving you the key back." I told him my dream was to have my own health club. I told him I wasn't going to let him kill it. I told him I needed another month. He asked me if I had a new lease for another space. I told him no, that I had just lost my new lease, even before I signed it.

After a few more minutes that seemed like years, the bank president said he'd give me another three weeks, but only on two conditions.

First, by Monday morning he wanted a copy of the lease for my new space, and *second*, he wanted a rent check for $1200 to pay for the additional month in the old space he had rented to me for another month. It was a Thursday afternoon when he told me he wanted both... on Monday.

Wait, there's one more space...
I left the bank president's office and immediately drove to a new, small shopping center that had just been built. I saw a man walking around who turned out to be the general manager. Though he was able to show me the available spaces right on the spot, I saw nothing that would work.

I was getting back into my car when the general manager stopped me, saying, "Wait, there's one space I didn't show you." He had hesitated because he didn't believe the owner of the shopping center would let a health club rent the space he had in mind. But he showed it to me anyway.

The space was perfect.

He said he would call me Friday, the next day.

It was four o'clock Friday afternoon and I still hadn't heard from him. I had one hour left, so I called him. He said he'd call me back. One hour later he did, telling me that, though the owner was against putting a club into that space, his lawyer thought it was a good idea. He asked me when I would like to sign the lease, and at five-thirty I was at his office signing a lease for a total of $168,000.

My net worth at that point: $6700. I gave them $3800 of it when I signed the lease.

The next Monday morning I was able to give the bank president a copy of the new lease and a first month's rent check for $1200.

I had $1700 left to build a new health club.

I hired carpenters, plumbers, air conditioning people, electricians, and everyone else I needed in order to build it. *I never thought of failure.* I advertised like crazy, knowing I'd have thirty days to pay for the ads. People came in and joined. I took their money and paid whatever I owed with whatever I could.

Week after week the club improved and the membership built and built.

Three weeks later I was able to move my members from the old bank building to my new center. It wasn't even close to being finished, so I told the members I'd extend their memberships for as long as it took me to finish. Six months later I finished building the club.

It was paid off completely.

The first thing on my list had been accomplished!

Remember that I'd promised myself I'd read my list night and day? Well, I did, and now something was catching my attention.

The fourth goal on my list was to make $100,000 by the time I was twenty-five. The only problem, though, was that by the age of twenty-three I had never made more than $11,000. So one day I put a line through the $100,000 and replaced it with $60,000. I didn't know how I was going to make that much, either, but at least that figure wasn't as far away as the six-figure goal I'd set earlier.

I was still reading my list night and day when I turned twenty-four, and realized I had broken my own rules by lowering that figure. So I put a line through the $60,000 and put the $100,000 figure back.

The result: By the day I turned twenty-six I had saved exactly $100,000. Not a penny over or under. When I saw that, I realized anything was possible.

Over the next seven years I accomplished everything on my list. I had learned about the power of believing and never quitting.

These days my life is built around helping people understand that we're *all* capable of achieving whatever goals we're willing to work for.

Thank God I opened the drawer in that desk when I was twenty!

About the Author

Joe Cirulli, who's been featured on the cover of *Inc* magazine and regularly lauded in books about American business, is described in one business bible as "revered around the world for his work in the fitness industry... his health clubs in Gainesville have been ranked as some of the top facilities in the world," included in the top percentile globally for sales, management, and community service. In a compilation of wise sayings by the noteworthy, Joe is listed with Euripides, Emerson, and Victor Hugo. Not bad for a guy who once had twelve cents to his name. Joe says he's focused his life on two things: "Helping people become healthy and building a company culture that inspires people to become their best." With his staff, he has accomplished many goals, including making and keeping Gainesville, Florida "The Healthiest Community in America."

Visit ghfc.com.

"I Never Wanted You," My Mother Calmly Said

Marilyn Sabini Gansel

"I never wanted you," my mother said to me casually one day, as she was brushing my hair.

Though the statement came out of the blue, as if it were an afterthought, the message hit home. *I was also an afterthought.* Unanticipated. Something that could not be prevented.

I must have been only three or four when I heard *"I never wanted you.* When I found out I was pregnant, I went to the doctor and told him, 'Remove it... use a coat hanger, whatever.' But I'm glad I have you. In the end, I'm glad."

There are some things you never forget. No matter how many "buts" you hear later. No matter how many apologies follow, you never forget the words, "I never wanted you."

Those words fueled every thought I had about myself throughout my life.

There I was: unworthy. A reject to be tossed aside for someone more valued, more loveable. *Anyone.*

The family that preys together

It wasn't just Mother. As a child I was repeatedly subjected to family members' cruel rejection. I was never embraced by any of them, physically or emotionally, and I was haunted by the question "Why?" I wasn't an ugly child, but I felt unattractive. No wonder. How attractive can you feel when you are not just ignored, but invisible? I had dark hair and brown eyes like my parents, but I always saw my hair as mousy brown and wildly untamed. My mother would brush and set it regularly, continually running after me with a comb in her attempts to fix me. I hated that never-ending fixing, which just reaffirmed what my gut was telling me: I just wasn't good enough.

Though I had an endearing smile, it's no wonder I didn't always feel like smiling. I was not a part of them. I was in the way.

My mom, dad and I first lived in an upstairs apartment above the Seaview Tavern in Stamford, Connecticut. Rats toured the yard from time to time, and roaches pushed through crevices in the floor in order to feast in our cupboards. Noise from the bar scene below could be clearly heard in our flat above.

Things improved, sort of. After my brother was born, we moved to a two-bedroom first-floor apartment across from the bar—a Victorian, so the four of us no longer had to sleep in our one bedroom. In the new apartment, my brother and I slept in a tiny room off my parents' bedroom.

But we were not alone. It was a compound, and I grew up surrounded by relatives who filled the other homes on the same property. There was a yellow ranch-style home that belonged to Joe, Marge, and their son, Joey. The house next to it that faced Cummings Park was occupied by my Aunt Elbina and Grandmother Nona. Behind and next to that house was a gray Victorian dwelling with front and back porches and a large two-to-three-car detached garage. The house had three levels and so offered three separate apartments for other family members, uncles and aunts Dave and Betty and John and Marie and of course our family, on the Victorian's first floor.

Finishing the job the family began

It may sound cozy, with shared holidays, children playing together, but the adults barely tolerated each other. I learned very early to interpret the ever-present, ongoing innuendos, including little whispers about my mother's implied failings. I felt my family's exclusion, some of it based on jealous feelings toward my mother. Instead of welcoming Mom into the family, they chose to automatically dislike her, to find fault wherever they could. One rumor was that my father's family thought I was born too soon, that perhaps Mom was pregnant before marriage. Sure, Mom was flirtatious, perhaps a bit on the wild side, a hairdresser who loved a good time—dancing, drinking, and smoking. She contributed to her own reputation, and they latched on to anything at all that would discredit her. Needless to say, those rumors sparked fireworks between Mom and Dad at home. Tempers flew on a regular basis, and family resentment filtered down till it reached me, a very vulnerable target.

I didn't speak much during those years, knowing that whatever I said would hardly be congruent with family politics. My viewpoints had been shouted down often enough in the past, in the same way as we were *all* shut out.

Finally I finished the job the family began, and shut myself down entirely.

Since my own feelings of unworthiness were intensifying, I chose at a young age to seek silent dreaming as my escape from the dread word, "unwanted." I kept busy envisioning myself somewhere else entirely, living a different life. I dreamed of a life of adventure, pretty clothes, and exotic vacations, but I also imagined myself doing something good for people, helping them in some way.

I was escaping, not only from my home life, but from the rejection I was also feeling in elementary school because of my learning disabilities. Those were days of ignorance when it came to diagnosing and teaching methods, so the label they gave me was "slow learner." I was assured by teachers that I would never go to college, and for a time I truly believed that.

I was, after all, a failure. I was so timid that I could never answer questions in class without shaking and trembling. My heart would pound and, weakly, I would try to answer. It was always a struggle to just keep up.

This Catholic high school was made worse than it might have been by the particularly cruel nature of the nuns in charge. Once, in grammar school, I made the unspeakable mistake of crawling to the front of the classroom to see a boy I liked, and paid for it by suffering a punishment geared to terminally humiliate any youngster. I was publicly dumped into a garbage can. And then there were other times during elementary school when I was brought up to the front of the room to be ridiculed, or to have my knuckles rapped with a ruler. During my stay at the private all-girl's Catholic high school, I would be ordered to let my hair down in front of everyone when I came to school wearing a bun, to save time after school when I attended ballet class.

This Catholic high school was an amazingly ascetic place—no dances, no boys, no fun, no proms, just hard work, prayer and penance. Even bathroom privileges were unnaturally restricted, resulting in permanent damage to my bowel functions. We were lively young girls trapped in a nun-like existence, ordered to walk down the right side of the hallways in silence in a line with hands folded in prayer, ordered to chapel at the start of each day, with nuns patting us down to be sure we were wearing girdles! I was not the only one singled out for chastisement, yet my shyness, my timid nature seemed to warrant the most abuse.

I felt unwanted by my mother, by my family, and now by my school.

The pattern had been set, and so it continued. Humiliated and rebuffed by failed romantic relationships, I escaped by picturing myself alone. Who would want me? I found comfort in food, eating to fill up the empty spaces in my life. I gained weight, only to prove further that I was ugly, imperfect, and worthy only of being unwanted. Embarrassed by my appearance, Mom put me on many diets, and I'd lose some pounds, then gain them back.

The abuse never seemed to let up. When I started as a practice teacher at a local high school, I was ridiculed by men (including my dad and brother) for having "a big ass." My self-esteem plummeted even further. I did find young men who were interested in me, but they were, according to family and the Sisters of the Presentation of Mary, the "wrong" type. They were not Christian, they were not Italian, they were *not good enough*. So now *they* weren't wanted, either!

Would God even want me in Heaven?

I had hit bottom. Slowly I began asking myself *Who were these people I was allowing to determine my happiness?* They were my family and my religion. As I started to look squarely at their authority, doctrines, and wisdom, I slowly began to question my own faith.

Since I was raised Roman Catholic, I learned to pray by rote—the Hail Mary, the Our Father, and the Rosary. But they were all just words without meaning. An innocent child has no idea what sin is, so in confession I learned to confess sins I never committed, saying the penance prayers eagerly, hungry for acceptance in any form.

As a Catholic, I was well educated in fear, beginning with the unspeakably cruel fear of Purgatory and Hell. Would God want me in heaven with Him? Was I good enough? Could I ever measure up to His standards? Well, my track record wasn't great, was it? Will I be damned? Contritely, I prayed for forgiveness and approval—for what? I really had no idea.

I began to notice contradictions and conflicts. I remember bringing a Jewish girlfriend with me to St. Mary's Catholic Church one Sunday. We might have been eight years old at the time, sitting in this magnificent gold-inlaid church with its huge stone altar. Its vastness swallowed us up. How tiny I felt then.

194

We listened to the Mass in Latin, and then, after the sermon was delivered in English, my friend whispered to me, "So, Marilyn, this means that because I am Jewish, I cannot go to heaven?" She looked really frightened by the priest's message about baptism and heaven. I was equally appalled. "No," I told her. "God is *your* Father, too. You will have a place in heaven." If she couldn't go there, I didn't want to go either. I was angry at this injustice and rejection. And then it hit me: "But Jesus was Jewish!" This revelation clearly defined a moment of truth for me. Heaven is for everyone!

My search for truth began that day. I went on to question all authority figures, the Vatican, the nuns and priests, relatives, and my parents. Being put down now no longer caused me to suffer in silence. I started speaking up, though not as loudly at home or with relatives as I did elsewhere: After all, my family could have written and starred in *The Sopranos*, they hadn't changed. They were still people bent on "an eye for an eye" retaliation. Instead, I sought answers in the wider world, investigating inequality and women's rights, abortion, war, and injustice wherever I found it.

After high school, I was rejected by college admissions offices; later the same held true for a Master's program. I never tested well, that's just the truth. But I started re-crafting my beliefs, visualizing myself successful, worthy, and with a purpose. I needed to prove myself to the college admissions departments that it was worth it to give me a chance, so I summoned up courage, stepped out of my comfort zone, and changed my mind-set to believe in me—worthy, loved, and valued. Because of my persistence, I was accepted on probation and I graduated with a BS and MS in Education with 3.0 and 3.5 averages.

Allowing rejection to strengthen me

As I reframed my perspective and trusted in a new story of acceptance, I started to replace my own handed-down familial tale of woe. My new story was mine and I was evolving. The nuns were wrong!

I found God after our daughter was born in 1976. I found a Father who was considerably different than the one I had grown up with. I found a forgiving Father, a loving Father, and a Father who wanted me, even when at times I didn't want Him. It was my new Father's loving message of forgiveness and acceptance that helped me feel worthy.

One important thing I learned during this powerful journey was that I had to forgive and love myself first before I could truly forgive and love others. Loving myself is still not easy, but I am a work in progress; I now understand that if I accept others first, it's easier to love myself. Focusing less on *me* and concentrating on loving others unconditionally strengthens my resolve to believe that I am also loved, even if love does not come from family or those closest to me. Rejection has given me the strength to rewrite my story and my beliefs, and in doing so I have found my purpose in life. Changing my attitude and being grateful for the blessings I already have help me deal with my unworthy feelings.

Funny, though, the painful old "unwanted" mantra still crept in when I least expected it—when I thought *I've got it under control.* It would continue to haunt me from time to time, even though I now understood its origins. Every once in a while it *still* rears its ugly head and shouts, "I'm still here. You *are* unworthy. No one wants you. You are nothing." So I have to revisit that old story and rip out some pages and make corrections. The edits are sometimes agonizing, but if I am honest and make the changes needed, I can read my new story with confidence.

Maybe these challenges of mine are the reason why I found solace in subconsciously designing a life around the unwanted. Now that I better understand the Law of Attraction and the inner workings of my belief system, I see that my life path has centered on surrounding myself with people who might appear "less than," or perhaps "invisible" to the human soul and eye. I have attracted unnoticed people and they have been attracted to me. I am a reflection of them, and they of me. I made all kinds of friends in college, including transvestites, homosexuals, and the "less physically attractive" men and women in Boston, where I went to school. I found friends of different races, creeds, religions, and ethnicities. I found thinkers and doers. I marched for causes and delighted in learning about the struggles of people and the way they overcame. I learned about injustice and discovered the power to fight for people's rights.

When I became a teacher, I was asked to teach students from poorer neighborhoods whose grades reflected failure and whose home lives showed signs of distress and agony. These were often angry young people whose lives, while somewhat different than mine, were very much like mine. These were the forgotten, the invisible, the unloved and unwanted. They might have had trouble learning, but they were bright; if given the tools to succeed, I knew they could. They needed vehicles with which to express themselves, and they found them by studying Black literature, acting in creative dramas, and empowering themselves to make decisions and become accountable. They became mine to love, nurture, and cherish. They were mine to supervise. They were mine to see flourish as they became productive members of their community.

I didn't need to see their past academic records. I didn't need to hear all the mistakes they made. I didn't need to hear how many times they were arrested for possession of narcotics. I just needed *them* and they needed *me*. They, too, were going to have the chance to create a new story where they could feel loved and be successful, even when obstacles show up at their door, because there will always be barriers that try to keep us from being who we are becoming.

My old story of the *unwanted, unlovable, and pitifully silent child* was an experience it was clearly in the cards for me to have, though that is not what I would have chosen for myself. Even today, as an adult, remnants of learned behaviors can bring back to me the pain of unworthiness when people tell stories about who they think I am or what I have done—people who say they know me and do not. Just like my mom, who dealt with lies about herself, there will be untruths and more hurts aimed at me, since family remains family. To say at such times that I do not feel pain or agony when someone lashes out or tries to make me feel unworthy or unwanted would be a lie. I still hear the "I never wanted you" voice. But I know now that it is because of my pain that I have purpose and passion. It is because of my struggles and my own longings for truth, acceptance, and forgiveness that I have compassion for others, love unconditionally, can share in someone's hurt, and can help others feel wanted, worthy, and loved.

I don't think I would be capable of any of this if I had not heard my mother say "I never wanted you" as she calmly brushed my hair.

About the Author

Marilyn Gansel, PsyD, is a sports psychologist, life coach, and educator who assists her clients, some of whom consider themselves the forgotten, the invisible, the unloved and the unwanted, to discover the authentic truth about who they are, their values, strengths, and inner longings.

She helps individuals explore their actions,

thoughts, and feelings, to dispel the inner voice that tells us we are not "good enough" or "smart enough."

As a coach she challenges clients working with their inner critics to release their powerful, destructive thoughts and feelings, turning obstacles into opportunities and possibilities. She expands their thinking and helps them to evolve through self-discovery and compassion, thus creating new stories.

Dr. Gansel is available for workshops and seminars as well as one-on-one or group coaching by phone or in person.

www.drmlifecoach.weebly.com

drm@drmlifecoach.com

How I Dared the
Demonic Duo

Joe Leonardi

Where did it all start? How did I become a raging food addict, specializing in sugar and carbs? And why did I, with all my experience, expertise, and education, ever allow my life to get so far out of control?

What's more, how did I let that happen *twice?*

The answer is simple. I was hiding! The bigger I got, the more true that was.

To fully understand my personal mystery, it was necessary for me to delve into my own psyche, a place that I must admit I had successfully avoided for most of my adult life. I was hiding from the world, sure, but most important, I was hiding from *myself.* At times the veil around me was composed of lard layers. At the other extreme, massive musculature did the trick.

But always the cloak was made all the more impenetrable by boisterous, blusterous bravado.

With these highly effective veils I hid the truth from everyone, starting with myself. I recall a time—I must have been twenty-one or twenty-two, because I was living in Hawaii—when the woman I was involved with ended our relationship, saying something very poignant. "I don't want to end this, but I can't stay with someone I don't know. Just share with me *the real you.*"

Looking back, I see that my response, pathetic though it was, was as sincere an answer as I could give at the time. I said to her, "If I knew the real me, I would."

I had buried "me" so far down that I didn't know who I was, and I certainly had no idea *why* I was such a mystery to me. I had to reach middle age, and bottom out a second time, to discover what caused me to conceal myself.

I am neither a psychologist nor a psychiatrist. I am a chiropractor, an educator, primarily a physical culturist.

I am someone who has on two occasions tipped the scales at a ponderous, pachydermian and unhealthy three hundred and forty pounds. Oh I know how to drop weight and get in shape, all right. I have the secret. I have shared it with others and I will share it here with you—are you ready?

Eat a diet as close to nature as possible, *exercise* seven days a week and keep positive mental *energy*. It is what I like to call the Three E's.

You see, my difficulty wasn't that I didn't have the knowledge; it wasn't even that I didn't apply that knowledge. After all, I had previously dropped to a healthy weight from *over* three hundred and forty pounds, and I did it with relative ease!

The problem lay in sustaining my weight loss. I was unable to do that because I simply hadn't realized why I had gotten so far out of control in the first place. That understanding only came after I bottomed out for the second and final time.

The terrible team meets the troubled trio
This time the second of the demonic duo appeared. The first time I slew my demon I only had one of them to battle, and that was food. The second time

food brought his disreputable brother to the table—alcohol. Together, the deadly duo teamed up to decimate my body and almost exterminate my existence.

It would be easy to blame the demonic duo, and just stop there, but that would be dishonest. The simple truth is that it was a troubled trio—me, myself and I—who fell for their allure. As my life crumbled, I became more vulnerable, beginning with a misdiagnosed illness that kept me out of my practice for several months. Then there was surgery. Then the surgery produced an undiagnosed infection that could very well have killed me. This drained my life savings, which in turn contributed to my marriage falling apart. Oh, and I neglected to mention that during this same period of time I lost a run for Congress.

And to top it all off, both my parents passed away.

My natural way of dealing with these terrible days was to use a sugar high to keep me awake for days, then to depend upon booze's powerful depressant to soak my brain and give me some semblance of sleep.

Like so many other life-threatening conditions, the duo came with rewards. One "benefit" of the demonic duo was that they allowed the layers of insulating, isolating, indolent lard to return, to do their job of protecting me from the world. This worked very well:

I couldn't fit into restaurant booths, so I took most meals alone.

I lacked the confidence needed for dating, so I spent nights alone.

I was unable to participate in any activities, so I spent my free time alone.

Well, not really alone—there were always my "friends," the demonic duo who remained faithfully nearby. I continued to hang out with them for longer and longer periods.

I could not see this at the time, but my self-destructive behavior, by itself, had nothing to do with the bad things that occurred in my life. It was my response to these situations that did the damage. It was I who chose gluttony and sloth as coping mechanisms. No one held my mouth open and forced the demonic duo down my gullet.

It was my choice to purchase and consume. It was my choice not to exercise. And, in the end, it was my choice to become obese.

An unforgettable, regrettable scene

I can't, nor do I ever desire to, forget one particular Saturday morning in October of 2007. I awoke from my usual drunken slumber to find two empty whiskey bottles and a third started. I don't know why I didn't die, but I didn't. Unable and unwilling to move, I sat for what seemed an eternity.

My awakening took place when I started shaking my head over and over again, asking myself *Why?* I thought about my parents and what they would think if they were still alive. I thought about my nephews and wondered how they would react when they one day learn that Uncle Joe allowed weakness and stupidity to take him away from them.

Something had definitely shifted.

I grabbed the third bottle and completely emptied the amber liquid—into the sink. I placed the now-empty bottle atop my refrigerator, the resting spot it still occupies to this day.

That was the end of one-half of the demonic duo's power over my life.

My issues with the other half didn't end that day, however. Handling my food addiction would take several more months. But I was starting at the only place I was able to start: with the way I was living day-to-day. First I found three suits that I could barely squeeze into and took them to the dry cleaner. I had resolved that it was time to end my slovenly dressing. Even if my body wasn't yet able to project pride in appearance, my attire could and would.

I started paying attention to other areas of my life again, as well. Instead of retreating to the squalor of my empty apartment every evening, I made a conscious decision to go out in public, even if it meant just meandering about a store. It was at one of these meanderings that I met my current girlfriend. Not really all that confident in myself, I saw Donna, someone with whom I was acquainted and always had a little thing for. I threw caution to the wind and asked her out on a date. I was shocked when she said yes.

I was living again! But I was still relying on what I considered, for me, to be the most evil of the demonic duo—food. While I may only have had one or two drinks socially during the next several months, gorging on food was still the name of the game, from the moment I trudged out of bed in the morning, to the moment I fell back into it in the evening.

That is, until one day in March (March 1, 2008, to be exact). I was climbing the stairs to my second-floor apartment when I realized something that I viewed then and now as wretched news. When I was only about halfway up the dozen steps to my apartment I had to pause to catch my breath.

This was it: the two-by-four to the head that I had needed. When I finally completed my ascent, I immediately stripped off my clothes. I then searched out the bathroom scale, now dust-covered, and cleaned the glass from the tell-tale window. I took a moment to gather my courage before mounting, and then hopped upon the truth-telling machine. I could hear the springs moan and groan as they responded to the heft they were being asked to register. I peered down, but much to my dismay I was unable to see the numbers hidden by the beach ball ballooning from my abdomen. So I inhaled with gale force power and sucked in my gut.

As I steadied myself, the needle bounced back and forth before settling on 3-4-0.

Obviously a broken scale, playing tricks
I jumped back in horror, not wanting to accept what

the scale had just told me. *This device must be out of calibration.* That was it. That was the answer. I would prove it by scouring my closet till I came upon an old forty-pound dumbbell, which I placed on the scale. I anxiously waited to be told the weight was eighty pounds. No such luck. The indicator stopped, spot on at 4-0.

It's kind of funny how the brain will play tricks. I didn't stop fantasizing there, but took it a step further, thinking to myself, "Well, I have worked out with heavy poundage most of my life, so I must still be holding plenty of muscular weight. Yeah, that's it." Now, of course I left out the fact that until I lifted that dumbbell, it had been almost three years since I had hoisted any weights or set foot in any gym.

But my denial wasn't dead *even yet.* When I next arrived at my office, I asked my office manager to take photos of me from the front and the side. I transferred them to my computer, fully expecting a big, powerful person to appear on the screen. What I saw was a pin-sized head atop a soft, rotund, pear-shaped body grinning back at me. Reality can hit you subtly, or it can be a cold, heartless bastard. On that day it was the latter. Reality finally hit home, and hard. So hard that I closed my office door and sobbed. I could not believe what I had allowed to happen—again.

But reality, the bastard, had excellent timing. I *was* ready, after all. After a brief period of self-pity, I took out three sheets of paper. On the top of one I wrote, EATING. On the next I penned EXERCISES. And atop the final one I wrote mental

ENERGY. I then filled out each page with plans to reclaim my health, wellness, and fitness.

Around noon of that day I walked across the hall to my doctor and she gave me a physical, including an EKG. Next, I drove over to my old gym and reactivated my long-dormant membership. On the following day I began my journey back from fat then to fit now.

But I knew there was one more piece of the puzzle I had to solve: I had to discover *why* I chose to respond to life's difficulties with food.

After my workout the following Saturday, I went for a long drive, and at the end of it I parked my car at one of my favorite spots, a secluded lake where I had spent many summers. I'd always found it a good place to think. And that's what I did, revisiting my childhood and calling up the time when I first started utilizing food as a coping mechanism. It was a painful process, but necessary. Even today, as I type these words and the scene comes back to me, I still have strong emotions.

I was very young, about ten years old, when my grandmother, known as "Mama" to the family, lived across the street. I would stop to visit most days, and she'd give me a little treat. Then she started to have memory issues. One day I came to the door and she didn't know who I was, telling me to "Go away, I don't know you." Of course, these days most of us would realize what was happening, but to a child at that time, it was completely baffling. And painful.

My grandmother continued to decline and, for whatever reason, my aunts and uncles determined that it would be my family who would move in to her house to take care of her. I am the youngest of all my male cousins; the closest in years to me is four years older, and the majority of them are at least ten years older. Most of my cousins were in college, but it was us kids, too young to understand and much too young to cope, who were uprooted and thrown into a situation few children would ever be able to understand.

Grandma loses her mind, and my trust

It was frightening for me to watch my beloved grandmother go from complete lucidity to moments of utter confusion, at times moving into total delusion. It was one of these delusional days that changed everything for me.

When I arrived home from school that day, my mother told me that my grandmother was having a good day. I was excited, since it meant that we would have the kind of visit I remembered and cherished. I ran into her room and gave her a kiss on the cheek. She smiled at me—I can still see the smile—but suddenly I saw instant terror on her face as she gripped my wrists in a threatening way and with a shocking amount of strength.

She wouldn't let go. Her grip was so tight that my hands were getting cold; I can feel that sensation now as I type these words. She shushed me and loudly whispered words that caused my young heart to skip several beats.

"That woman in the kitchen, she is going to take you down to the cellar. She is going to chain you there and kill you!"

I begged.

I pleaded.

I sobbed and struggled to free myself.

But my grandmother would not let go; instead she repeated that terrifying threat. Even after my mother, hearing my sobbing, rushed in, my grandmother would not listen to her. She only clamped down harder. My mother called my father at work and, as he had done so many times, he clocked out immediately and rushed home. For whatever reason, my grandmother always recognized my father, and as soon as she saw him she calmed down and let go of me.

Everyone thought this disturbing incident was finally over then, but for me it proved to be just the beginning.

I snuck down to the cellar that night to check each room for the chains. For years I had nightmares and, even to this day, barely a week goes by that I don't recall the events of that day.

Eventually my grandmother passed away and, as often occurs, a nasty squabble among her children developed. I even overheard one uncle call my father a criminal, claiming that we stole from her.

The only thing stolen was a big part of my childhood.

I finally remembered this life-altering incident, this key to the riddle, as I sat there by my childhood lake. *So that's when I turned to my food for comfort and solace!* The painful memories eventually became even clearer. On Sundays I would take whatever money I had to buy candy, cupcakes, and soda. Settling into my bedroom, I would watch football all day while munching on my snacks. On other days, I would lose myself in comic books or other sedentary activities, all the while eating junk food and gaining weight.

From then on, the battle to lose weight grew into a daily struggle, as I swung from one extreme to the other: either overweight or overly muscular, the two extremes I successfully used to hide myself from the world.

Once I finally found the key, I knew I would no longer lose weight for appearance sake alone, any more than I would gain muscle for reasons of either intimidation or isolation. I would recapture my fitness for one reason alone, to improve my health. I would understand that what happened, happened and I would be stronger than my circumstances. I would now choose how to respond to good and bad times.

The goal was not to simply *undo my obesity*. It was to become healthy. I realized, after all these years, that weight loss is a side effect of fitness, fitness is not the end result of weight loss.

Most important, I confronted my demonic duo, conquered them, and now I live the life I was meant to live.

About the Author

With a BS from the University of the State of New York and a Doctor of Chiropractic degree from New York Chiropractic College, Joe Leonardi is an adjunct faculty member at Luzerne County Community College. He has acted as the team chiropractor for the Arena Football League 2's Wilkes-Barre/Scranton Pioneers, as well as the semi-professional Scranton Eagles and NEPA Miners football teams and the women's roller derby Coal City Rollers. He has also provided chiropractic care at powerlifting and Strong Man events. Leonardi has made numerous television, radio, and Internet appearances to discuss the topics of fitness, wellness, obesity, childhood obesity, and the relationship of childhood obesity to bullying.

He is the author of *Obesity Undone: Fat Then Fit Now, A Life Beyond Weight Loss* and *Sometimes the Bastard Returns: A True Life Account of Obesity Relapse,* which can both be found on Amazon.com. His web site is FatThenFitNow.com and he can also be reached at FatThenFitNow39@gmail.com.

Part Five

What the Tragedy Taught Me

The Gift Horse

Cathleen Halloran

Cigarettes and tropical fruit?

I know that smell.

An involuntary roll of my body meets the weight at the end of my bed. Slowly I lift one eyelid, spying out from behind the flesh curtain. My visual perspective is so askew, my eyelashes seem like branches in the foreground.

Trying to focus, realizing *I know her.* Her smoky musk makes me smile.

I must like her. I flip through my mental rolodex, perplexed by its emptiness... I just keep flipping.

There she sits, probably one of the longest friendships I have had... *and yet...*

I don't move, I just stare, gather information, and smile. She realizes I am awake and begins to talk. It is slowly coming together.

In a scratchy whisper I ask, "What happened?"

She shuts the phone in her hand with a loud snap after an abrupt ending to her conversation, sticks a pen behind her ear, and responds: "You had a horse riding accident."

Even now, the air around this girl... Julie... is all busyness. Now I remember how much she worked!

Not only am I talking in a scratchy whisper, I talk so slowly! I spit out, "It must have been a bad accident for you to be here."

She laughs and says, "I have been with you every Tuesday since April."

Staring is the only response I can give her.

"You almost bit it! I came directly to Hartford Hospital right when Andrus called me. This place is nicer, less sterile."

Julie tells me about my horse riding accident.

"Whose horse?"

"Yours. That free one you just got."

Free one? I have no idea.

I can't remember why I am unable to move, how I got here, wherever *here* is. I use my left hand to pick up my right hand. It all seems so unfamiliar. *A free horse?*

The whirlwind unwinds

Currently it is June. Apparently I had a riding accident in April (my horse fell, not me!).

It was an Easter Monday, and it started like most of my days.

I was going to take a lesson on my new "free" horse. (Did you ever hear "There's no such thing as a free horse"?) Ms. O'Malley was going to be my new event mount. We only had four weeks until our first competition.

It was a brisk, dewy spring morning. I needed to get going early.

Owning my own business, a clothing company, was rewarding and demanding. Every day I had a long to-do list. This week was going to start out with a trip to the city to retrieve my clothing and accessories from a fashion show we had just participated in. First things first.

Monday, April 17th to-do list:

1) Take a lesson on my new horse.
2) Deposit money in the bank to cover the check I wrote to the IRS.
3) Stop at my new store to check paint colors and progress of renovation.
4) Stop in Millbrook to drop off custom jacket to a client.
5) Stop at factory and check new production.
6) Go to the cutting room to see if the next lot is ready.
7) Pick up samples from fashion show.
8) Get new buttons, new trim.

Just a typical day, which lent itself well to my being a chronic speeder. Take note of "the check to the IRS"—doing things backwards, writing checks and then looking to see if there is enough money. I loved being on the edge, addicted to chaos, the chaos that would ensue after I bounced checks and got speeding tickets.

I was designing, producing, selling, taking orders, and sometimes filling them all at once.

My studio was a mess! I designed the same way I wrote checks—backwards! I would buy fabric and buttons that I loved and then make something out of them. I had a financial business partner who made this possible, so I was able to design what I wanted. I was having a really good time!

My life felt like a whirlwind. Until it came to a complete halt.

On April 17th I never got past the first thing on my to-do list.

After my accident I was in a coma for five weeks and then in Gaylord Hospital for two months of treatment for a traumatic brain injury.

My husband, Gabriel, would assure me that it was all just temporary—the wheelchair, the adult diaper, my right eye that was pointed in the wrong direction and causing double crooked vision, the paralysis on the right side of my body.

Our lives had been too busy with work and our separate hobbies for us to spend time together. *This* brought us together. Gabe took charge of overseeing my care.

Meanwhile, I would just laugh. One of the side effects of my brain injury was what I refer to as emotional incontinence. I laughed all the time! Often at completely inappropriate times. For most of my life I didn't take things too seriously. In fact, at high school graduation I wasn't elected Most Likely to Succeed or Best Looking, I was voted Class Clown. I never was known for my mature nature, and now... definitely not.

When you almost "bite it" is when you really put things in perspective.

You ask, "How important is it?"

It is true that every brain injury is different. It all depends on where you hit / or get hit in the head. I must have knocked just the right spot in my little brain. Often people wake up from comas with emotional incontinence in the other direction—yelling, swearing, angry. In fact, the doctors warned Gabriel that I might wake up really angry, and would need to be medicated.

Not me! I woke up laughing.

It must be hard to determine what is going on in the brain of a coma patient.

My unconventional sign of life

This is how my story was relayed to me:

For nine days they did not know if I was brain dead or not. On the day of my accident, I was taken by helicopter to Hartford Hospital. The first diagnosis was grim. Gabe was told, "I don't see any good outcome here," by the on-call doctor. Gabe hated that answer, so he had my doctor switched.

My sister Maureen later told me, "You arrived at the hospital at level 3, meaning no verbal, eye, or motor response, diagnosed a traumatic brain injury with diffuse axonal injury and brain stem trauma. Prognosis was not optimal. You also presented with alternating decerebrate and decorticate posturing and remained at level 3 for several days, with your score climbing slowly after a week. They kept you sedated for healing purposes at around week two," blahblahblah.

There were constant attempts to get me to respond. Lights, noise, talking, were all prompts to see if I was still in there. I had also contracted "hospital pneumonia," which caused me to retain fluids, so I blew up! I got *huge*. Gabe had to take my wedding bands off my ever-puffing fingers. If he had waited any longer, the rings would have to have been cut off.

One of my first signs of life was giving a relative the finger after she made a joke about how my wrinkles had disappeared from being so bloated and I would no longer need Botox. Although I remained in a comatose state, paralyzed on the right side of my body, I still seemed to remember the ongoing joke between us, which was that she thought I should start with a "Botox maintainance program," despite the fact that I love being able to contort my fair Irish sun-damaged skin into scowls. So flipping her the bird, comatose or not, would have been a completely appropriate answer to what she said.

Astonished, Gabe said, "You just gave my sister the finger! Did you mean to?" Of course I did. So I did it again. After this coming out party I remained in various states of coma for weeks.

Wrong girl in the kitchen
I was shuffled around Gaylord from doctor, to therapist, to group sessions, and began regaining motor skills. I learned to walk again, practicing on stairs. I was talking, very slowly, and was fitted with a pair of prism glasses. When a few more basic skills were in

place, we were brought to a makeshift kitchen.

I asked the therapist, "What are we doing in here?"

Theresa, in her soft musical voice, said, "It's to help us get prepared for being at home, to get reacquainted with cooking utensils and equipment."

I assured her, "I don't need this, I was not in the kitchen *before* my accident!" That was confirmed by my always-nearby husband.

As a group, we would bake cookies from a box mix. The first batch had been removed from the oven—(by the therapist, after a patient tried to grab the hot tray without an oven mitt)—and after it had cooled down, she offered them to us. When I politely refused, she said, "Cathleen, don't you want to try one of our cookies?" I said: "No way, I saw how they were made."

A kitchen full of brain patients don't make the most appetizing food.

I could smell the cookies, but my taste buds were still in a coma. I also never knew whether I was hungry or full. I completely relied on being fed.

At mealtimes my husband would wheel me into the dining room and tie a bath towel around my neck to act as a full body bib.

No horses named Halloran
I grew up in a middle-class, two working parents, big Irish Catholic family. Horses were not on the radar at the Halloran house. The country lifestyle at 24 Pleasant View in Beacon, New York, consisted

of grass stains on our pants, playing ring-and-run in the neighborhood, and our mile walk to parochial school.

But boy, could I dream!

Soon I was living my dream. Riding and owning horses. Making clothing with a label of my own, with freedom to design to my heart's content. We had beautiful catalogs, fashion shows, parties. I exhibited at trade shows, and magazines wrote articles about the line. I showed my collections during fashion week at Bryant Park in New York City, the first time exhibiting the collection in a horse trailer, which drew a lot of attention.

I tried to live the part. I had five horses that I cared for on a daily basis. I was ultimately responsible for my company, which included designing, selling, and producing the lines through an O'Halloran retail store and a mobile store. I managed a group of amazing employees! We made custom clothing, home furnishings, and horse blankets.

Any one of those things would be a full time job.

Waking up in the morning, I would throw my legs over the side of the bed and hit the floor running—literally, either going for a run or to chores in the barn. My days were about action, creation, motivation, and stress, but they always started with animals. I loved it!

My reality was an escape from reality.

Plans were in the works for a bigger store with a very grand Grand Opening. It was scheduled for

June with an over-the-top, funky fashion show, complete with circus acts.

More. My favorite drug was the drug of *more.*

I was staying so busy so I didn't have to look at myself. I wasn't even aware that I needed to look at myself. If I could keep all these balls in the air, what could possibly be the problem?

Doing laundry did not fit in with the busy image I wanted to have of myself. I would happily muck a stall… but laundry, not so much. Instead, I would buy new. New underwear, new socks, jeans, shorts.

More. Just *more.*

Then, one day I woke up, Now it's ALL new. I was the girl who was always the driver. I was the one you would ask to get your cat out of the tree. Now I need a shower chair. I fall over putting my underwear on and my morning coffee comes out my nose.

I didn't know much before, and I definitely didn't know how to do *this!*

I had heard tales from some Buddhist type friends about "making your bed." They swear that you should start the day by making the bed. I figured what the hell, I don't know what else to do with my day, I can't even go down the stairs to do laundry now! I never made the bed before, but I would give it a whirl. I found that making the bed is a bit difficult when you only have one working arm. I would make about sixteen trips around the bed to finish the task.

Making the bed changed my life.

This was it. I didn't have all of the things that

were once mine. Work, extreme sports (did I forget to mention the helicopter snowboarding and mountain biking?).

My horses. I felt a little naked without them.

I just kept making the bed.

Being dependent is a very humbling thing. People came out of the woodwork to help and I continued to get better. Acceptance was the answer to all my problems. I was grateful to be alive and did not get too frustrated, finding the humor, irony, and relief in my condition.

Relief! What relief? Really, *relief?*

A new life born in the here and now

I have spent my life trying to impress everyone. Trying to impress myself. It is a strange thing. I would say and do whatever I wanted, and would get so mad at you if you didn't like it!

I got married when I was young and newly sober. I had no idea who I was and had created a facade in my drinking days. I switched drugs to the one called "Being in Love" so I didn't have to grow up. I didn't expand the basic living skills that a girl might need. Instead, I just concentrated on the ones that everyone liked, the ones that seemed to work for me.

It worked. I just kept moving.

God sure is funny! After the accident, my life became so located in the here and now that I can remember the great feeling of success I had when I finally managed to open a door with my right hand. It required great practice and concentration, using a step-by step tutorial for my muscles. It went something like this... *OK, close your fingers... all of them! Hold. Now turn! YES!*

I would often be so excited about this trick that I would forget to tell my hand to let go, and would shut it in the door. My right arm was always covered with bruises.

It often felt like starting from scratch.

A clean slate.

I will forever be grateful to Gabriel for the care he took of me and my recovery after my accident. I couldn't have had a better person at my side. But we had longstanding and fundamental differences and, after a great deal of prayerful thought, I came to understand that I do not owe him the rest of my life.

I leaned into my God and my support network and saw that I need to grow up. I do not have the same skills and charm I did when I got married, so I need to develop real life skills.

When it was time to for me to leave my marriage, I trusted. I trusted because there had been an intervention in my life. I felt like the Universe said, "OK, Cathleen, you had a nice ride, I will give you a Get Out of Jail Free Card." My self-inflicted jail, that is.

It would have been "easier" to just stay married. It was safe. I knew it wasn't right.

I prayed my ass off.

Today I am with the love of my life. We're both enjoying double-digit sobriety and are married. Animals have come and gone in my life and I love each one and try to be the best animal mom I can be.

I live a dream beyond my wildest dreams. My days start with "Good morning GOD, thank YOU, and help me be of service to You today."

Then I make the bed.

Pretty simple.

I am so grateful to my God for the life I have, for giving me experience and courage. I just want to share it, and I do, wherever possible.

I suit up and show up, with a little grace and dignity, to just be present and available for what life brings that day.

About the Author

This is the first time Dutchess County, New York's heralded equestrian designer, now Cathleen Halloran McCallian, has told the story of her dramatic reinvention. A few months before the 2006 horse stumble that changed her life, *Women's Wear Daily* was triumphantly calling her collection "a small jewel." Halloran had, typically, grabbed the Bryant Park fashion world's attention by stationing liveried trumpeters outside her horse trailer/showroom. It worked. She was living up to the impressive reputation planted by, among others, *Country Living* magazine in 2005, as they called her "the quintessential horsewoman," praising her designs and describing her as "a tall, blue-eyed, redheaded beauty, to boot." To *Hudson Valley* Magazine, Cathleen Halloran, then owner of O'Halloran's in Millerton, New York, was, simply, "a sensation."

Cathleen Halloran McCallian is currently writing, hiking, painting, embracing her inner domestic goddess, loving on all of her animals, and delighting in married life.

She recently pulled out the sewing machine...

Darling Daughter

Mary Monahan

Dear Mom,

The card is a golden yellow color, bright, with purposefully frayed edges. You gave it to me when I was in eighth grade. Not sure what to make of it, I tacked it to the bulletin board in my office.

The front of it reads, "My Darling Daughter," followed by a generic description: "... beautiful and good, honest and principled, determined and independent, sensitive and intelligent..." I wondered if, when you picked out this card for me, you believed I really were those things, or if you instead believed that's what a Darling Daughter would look like if you had one.

Your first suicide attempt marked what I once believed to be a curse, my undoing, the beginning of an obsession ever-present in the back of my mind. The worst part looks like this: You knew, just like every mother knows her child, why I became the person I became at that time, the person we had never intended for me to be, and decidedly not the Darling Daughter. You flagged the part where I took the wrong road, your suicide attempt the juggernaut for everything that happened thereafter.

When other mothers were making sacrifices on what my friend refers to as "the altar of motherhood," you were praying to leave us.

People say that parents' love for their children is unconditional, but I have always believed it to be strictly the other way around. At least in our house.

The irony of it all is this: For your whole life you wanted to die, until you were given the final timeline, a year to live, and suddenly you were fighting for your life. I remember wondering if, after a lifetime of death wishes, you manifested a terminal illness, keeping in mind your frequent reminder to me:

Careful what you wish for because you may just get it.

Remember just a few weeks before you passed away, and we were watching the news when the toxicology reports deemed Heath Ledger's death an accidental overdose? The silence in the room was deafening, and it was as if you were being prompted to finally acknowledge the nightmare you knew had always chased me. You turned to me, your arm reattached to a prosthetic rib cage in the absence of a shoulder, having undergone a mastectomy, your voice slurry from morphine, to remind me that your overdose was an accident, too.

I could feel you willing it to be so. Though we both knew the truth. Aware that this was your misguided attempt to protect me, I chose to remain silent. In the same way that you knew how your suicide attempts affected me, you also knew that I didn't believe you.

You didn't believe you.

And isn't "accidental overdose" an oxymoron?

Two days before you died, when I knew you were gathering enough strength to go to the other side, I looked deep into your eyes and smiled. You smiled back during that rare, lingering moment of lucidity, and that one moment channeled a lifetime of forgiveness between us.

This was our unspoken amends to each other—I, for not being your Darling Daughter, and you, for not being my Dutiful Mother.

I believe we have a spiritual contract, Mommy. (It's funny how, now that you are dead and I am an adult, I sometimes refer to you as Mommy—I never would have before, even as a young child.) What I once blamed you for—a dark past, crippling shame, the alcoholism and addiction—I now see as a bright white light. I hold our past like a mustard seed in the palm of my hand. Waiting for its growth, I cradle it, swaddle it in love and forgiveness.

Always, there is the promise that something good will come from it all.

The last of your belongings left in the house after your passing was the photo of a tree with a caption below it. I remember that photo hanging in our living room. The elegant script juxtaposed against the harshness of the gnarled, bare tree reads: *No noble tree ever disowned its dark roots.* I never gave much thought to it.

Today I found that picture, left in the corner of a deep closet, everything else of yours gone, all of your belongings picked over, fought over, or judiciously divided—there it was. I knew you had been saving this last one just for me.

Love,
Your Darling Daughter

About the Author

Mary Monahan, raised in New England, holds Master's degrees in both writing and education. She is interested in all things having to do with transformation and resilience, and tries to live by Rumi's conviction that, "The wound is the place where the light enters you."

The Stairway Above

Jason Jean

My days consisted of waking up at five a.m., kissing my two girls' heads while they slept, grabbing a coffee on the road and then driving to my job sites. The days ended with grabbing a coffee on the way home, watching my headlights shine off the road, and kissing my kids' heads while they slept.

You never know when those kisses will end. Will they end as they grow older, and you are no longer Daddy, just Dad? Do they end when you are bothering them as they talk with their friends on the phone? Will someone else get those kisses as they are falling in love for the first time? Do the kisses end when they move on from what was once home to their own life?

For me, those kisses almost ended too early—in my life and in theirs.

Living for things I had no time to enjoy

I grew up watching my father work more than seventy hours a week to support our family over many years, and I built the same work ethic. It was this drive to succeed that clouded my judgment about what is important in life. I used to think it was the 5000-square-foot house, three cars in the driveway, motorcycles, four-wheelers, boats, and jet skis that showed you were a success. But as I amassed those things, and I use the word *things* loosely, I became less and less able to actually *use* them.

Here's how it went: Work more and more, use toys less and less, work even more, use toys even less. I never actually was able to see the pattern myself, and when it was suggested to me, it fell on deaf ears. Family and friends would make comments like, "Stop and smell the roses," or "Why have all those things, since you never use them?" Whether I used them or not, I owned them. It was a status thing for me, mentally.

Though my wife and I have always taught our children to be themselves and never run with the Joneses, I was actually guilty of not living by my own words. What I was doing was serving a life sentence to things, the very things we teach our children shouldn't be important in life.

For years our lives as a family ran on autopilot, five a.m. to nine p.m., seven days a week, 360 days a year. Russy was the glue that kept things together; she's a great mother, wife, and friend. We had three incredible babysitters, Jamie, Megan and Mandy, all Penn State students who actually felt more like family than babysitters, as they'd join us for family dinners, trips, and special occasions. But what was lacking was Dad, or Daddy. Were the few hours a week my family saw me enough? I assumed it was.

As the sun rose over the hilltops going down the highway, it shined bright, and I thought *What a great day*! Dressed in my jeans and my usual polo shirt, I made my way around to all my job sites for the day. As I pulled up to the final job for the day, with the sun just at the top of the trees, I thought, *It's almost over*. I made my way through that last construction site into the new home we were building and up to the second floor to talk to my supervisor, who was working on a porch roof.

After a little small talk, I looked at Keith, a close friend and site supervisor, and said, "Let's call it a night." He agreed. I said, "Here, give me that board, and I'll pull it in the window for you." As he handed me the 2x10, I grabbed hold so as not to get my clothes dirty, took two steps back, and fell through an open staircase, twenty-two feet to the basement floor below.

Can twenty-two feet change a life? Can a blink of an eye in time change one's personality forever? Can you, in a split second, realize for the first time what is important in life and what's not? I am living proof that you can and you will.

Moments after living through a life-changing experience like this, you are simply hoping you can move body parts, hoping you will be the same person you were before, thankful for even being alive, knowing you shouldn't be.

An accidental view of the Big Picture

Once the initial shock of what just happened starts to clear your mind, you have a quick *Why me?* thought. That thought didn't last long for me, personally. I was just so thankful to be alive. Falling that distance and surviving is one thing, but it's quite another thing to survive knowing my broken pelvis and spinal cord injury will heal and that, though I will never physically be the same, I will be okay.

I often thank God, not only for allowing me to survive, but for what also took place. I know that may sound weird, but if it hadn't been for that accident, I wouldn't have been able to see what I was missing. I was missing so much in life, because I was more worried about all the materialistic things and not what is really important, which is family.

I know it sounds like a cliché, but until you have a near-death experience, you have no idea what such an event would mean to you. This accident allowed me to see everything around me that I was missing: watching the kids eat breakfast and get ready for school, listening to what they did during the day—all the gifts I missed for all those years when I wasn't around. I often hear people who work my kind of hours argue, "Oh I'm not like that, I'm around." Then you ask their families, only to find out that in reality the people who think they "are around" are delusional.

Don't get me wrong, I've relapsed over time as my entrepreneurial inner me slowly tries to take over again, and the drive to be the biggest at whatever I'm doing tries to tempt me into working all the time. But I find I am able to quickly remember not to fall back into my old ways, especially when I wake up in the morning and find it tough to walk or move, which is more common when it rains or gets too cold. Those physical effects always will be a part of my new life—a reminder to stay true to the new me.

Lasting change means vigilance

The accident brought me another gift, as well. My life-changing experience gave me the ability to help others who want to be helped to see what is really important to them. I've been able to share, not only my personal healing from the accident, but the healing that took place with my family. In order for people not to feel they're all alone, it's important for them to hear that there are others out there like them who have had something similar or worse happen.

From my own experience I am also able to show others that this change in their lives won't last on its own, that we have to work to stay on the right path, that it's easy to fall right back into your old ways.

Our family has less than we did before, as far as the size of our home goes. We also have zero materialistic toys. Our focus is now on our children and their futures. My wife and I enjoy our time with each other more, especially when it comes to our children's activities.

I can't lie, I have to admit there are days when I miss all the work and the late hours. There's something about living that way, putting in a hard day's work, that makes you feel good when the day is over. To be honest, there are times when I find it tough playing the at-home dad, knowing that my professional growth has been restrained. These days I only allow my businesses to grow enough to keep me busy, which means I need to go easy on the traveling.

As a matter of fact these changes are sometimes tough on the whole family. Though I expect our kids to be very respectful and appreciative, our kids make us especially proud of the level of respect and appreciation they continually reach, not because they do what we tell them to do, but because they so often make the right decisions based on what we taught them about life.

As I've gotten older I become more and more capable of judging my success, not on car emblems anymore, but on the success of my children, my marriage, friendships, and health.

That's what my accident taught me.

About the Author

Jason C. Jean is the author of *Life's Tool Belt* and *I Will I Am I Was.* He is an award-winning athlete, entrepreneur, chef, motivational speaker, and life coach who teaches proven principles that work for anyone, in any situation, at any time.

Tempering Fires:
The Invisible Truth
That Set Me Free

Craig N. Piso

I was born and raised in Pittsburgh, Pennsylvania, in a middle-class suburban neighborhood with nice neighbors and good schools. I was four years old when my family moved from the city to the North Hills to live in the house built by my father. A master carpenter, he wanted to give us "a better life" than he and my mother endured as children. Both had been raised in impoverished environments during the Great Depression and had suffered tremendous family losses, abuse, and heartaches.

My three sisters and I were brought up in strict accordance with "Old Country" values and rules, such as "Children are to be seen and not heard." Both parents had been deeply wounded in their youth, leaving them largely self-absorbed, emotionally unavailable and insensitive, and much more interested in working for things than in being close to us as children.

We each learned early to walk on eggshells, sensing we were a burden and source of misery, trying hard not to provoke their frustration, anger, and punishment. By doing exactly what was expected, we avoided the verbal and physical abuse that loomed darkly like a threatening shadow. I became vigilant so as to anticipate my parents' negative moods, trying to stay one step ahead, reading their minds in order to avoid the pitfalls. But each of us invariably took turns coming up short, and each of us paid the price. If we behaved as if we had "a mind of our own," or otherwise failed to meet either parent's sternly rigid expectations, the torture resumed as they redoubled their efforts to bring us into alignment.

Touched, but not by love

"Spare the rod and spoil the child" became the regular, terrifying mantra that would precede the beatings I received with merciless cruelty, usually in front of my sisters, deepening my suffering through humiliation. Sadly, I have almost no memory of ever being touched by either parent in a way that did not bring physical and/or emotional pain. My emotional wounds continued to disturb me well into my adult years, long after the physical injuries had healed.

Though we lived in a clean, well-constructed house, family life was a disempowering and depressing existence. I frequently ran away—going as far as possible—accompanied only by my imagination, seeking adventures while hiking in the woods, bicycling for hours to explore new worlds, and immersing myself in activities that would bring at least temporary relief from my misery. Each pursuit provided a much-needed break from my unbearable feelings, especially the ones I felt upon re-entering the house at night.

Father had been raised in dire hardship by his alcoholic, abusive, and neglectful father—a "hunky" coalminer—and his alcoholic mother. Until his death he remained greatly ashamed of and angry at both. Since my father did embody many truly admirable traits and qualities when sober, I'm indebted to him for many of my strengths and abilities. But when he was drinking heavily he often became critical/judgmental, impatient, paranoid, verbally and physically abusive, demeaning, and embarrassing. He had been fighting his entire life against a world he perceived as having mistreated him, and was still having episodic fistfights in bars into his late forties.

Mother possessed many admirable qualities as well: keen intelligence, exceptionally high standards, and well-intended aspirations for our family. It was from her that I came to appreciate the importance of education as the key to self-empowerment. Having been a fine student herself, she instilled in me a commitment to my studies, spending time with me in the early years to ensure that I, too, would excel academically, in spite of my short attention span and hyperactivity. She was determined to exceed the culture and quality of life she ascribed to her family of origin—people for whom she had lifelong disdain and with whom she had minimal emotional ties.

In my mother's zeal for self-advancement and perfection, however, the strengths that usually served us well were often exaggerated till they became compulsions, causing suffering for all in the household. For instance, she placed an extremely high value upon cleanliness and organization, insisting that the house and children be free of dirt and clutter. But she overdid it, lacking empathy for us, and placing her own emotional needs in front of our own. Her intolerance for the normal inconveniences created by children—dirt, dishes, and disarray—overwhelmed and enraged her.

Remembering the unbearable

I have vivid memories of myself as a young child being bathed by my mother in scalding hot water, into which she had poured laundry detergent with bleach—asserting with self satisfaction that "Cleanliness is next to godliness," especially after my coming home in the soiled clothing she also resented having to wash. In her agitation, she ignored my tear-laden screams, my pleas for her to stop. My skin reddened as she poured steaming water over my head to rinse my hair, the laundry soap containing bleach burning my eyes. She showed me no compassion, not even a merciful respite from the unbearable torture. Instead, I received an even more vigorous burning rinse while being cracked on the head with a large stainless steel pot she always borrowed from the kitchen.

My feelings never mattered, because my mother could only relate to the world through the lens of self-absorption that characterized her personality.

Since her death at age eighty in 2008, I have forgiven my mother, but I will never forget a lifetime of disappointment at her failure to nurture me emotionally or to love me in the most fundamental ways mothers normally love their offspring.

I always struggled in school—too emotionally undeveloped, anxious, and traumatized to achieve my potential. Recognizing my struggle, my father would offer me $5 for any report card with all As and Bs, and $10 for a report card with nothing below A—a relative fortune for our family and, thus, a wonderful expression of the value that both parents placed upon education. I almost never missed receiving a cash reward, starting in elementary school and through high school, not because I wanted the money, but to get my parents' positive attention and approval, which, sadly, almost never came otherwise.

Sadness on the sidelines

To offset my feelings of worthlessness and despair, I was an enthusiastic athlete from early childhood, especially when it came to my passion, baseball. Through baseball I was able to elevate my self-image to the point that I actually believed I had the potential to become a great player. But my parents forbid me to join the Little League, not wanting to pay the fees or take me to practice or games. It depressed me to watch my neighborhood buddies going to their games, dressed in their colorfully numbered uniforms. They were part of the real thing, being given the opportunity to develop the same skills for which I thought I had the raw natural potential.

My long-awaited participation in organized athletics finally started in seventh grade, where I excelled in track and received affirmation and praise, briefly filling the emptiness within me. In tenth grade, needing to choose between track and baseball for my spring sport, I chose track, being too afraid to risk failure at my true passion, baseball, while clinging to ongoing success in my secondary sport. I simply couldn't afford to fail.

This decision became one of my great regrets. I wanted so much to emulate Roberto Clemente, my childhood hero, but instead I paid the toll for my unsettling fear. I had settled for the good instead of reaching courageously for what could have been greatness!

Struggling as a college sophomore, I changed my major from accounting to psychology, a milestone in my development, since that was the first time I willfully acted on my own behalf as an adult without parental permission. While that required courage, I dreaded telling my parents, even more than I feared approaching my academic advisor with the news. Though he had never berated or abused me, I had been primed to expect he would.

When I nervously told my parents my decision that weekend, my father insisted that I learn to burn metal with an acetylene torch and to weld, using the equipment he maintained in our backyard. He wanted to ensure that I'd be able to at least earn a living, since he was convinced my psychology career path would eventually fizzle. To say the least, I did not have their blessing, although their commitment to my education and long-term success, in general, never wavered.

Finally feeling free to chart my own course and strongly motivated to prove my parents wrong, I took every psychology course offered at Grove City College. Unfortunately, only my mother would be present at my college graduation.

Starting the year on thin ice
During my junior year Christmas break, I worked as a boilermaker alongside my father in order to pay

my tuition. The job was on the construction site of a water tower in Columbus, Ohio, a highly paid job, but very dangerous work, even on good days. New Year's Eve, 1974, was not a good day, with freezing rain and cutting winds, but the job foreman decided we would work anyway.

Upon hearing the foreman's decision, my father admonished me to be extra cautious as we both headed for the job, confidently predicting, "Someone's going to get hurt today." He knew from experience that every step would be like walking on a skating rink, since there was sure to be a glazed veneer of ice on each and every rung of a ladder that reached to a height of 120 feet. He also knew that numerous safety violations existed on this job, including failure to affix the safety cage surrounding the ladder that was welded to the tower's central pillar, making traversing that icy ladder even more dangerous.

Shortly after lunch, while working on a scaffold at 110 feet, I was interrupted when one of the guys yelled, "Pete fell!"

Pete was my father.

Figuring he had fallen from the scaffold above me, twelve stories high, I assumed my father was dead when I looked down to see him lying motionless on his back on a steel platform, appearing from that enormous height like a mere speck. Panic-stricken and traumatized, I made my way down eleven stories on that same treacherous ladder, knowing full well that I, too, could fall to my likely death if I did not proceed with extreme caution, but also knowing that my father awaited me below.

I felt overwhelming anguish as I fearfully re-strained my movements at every ladder rung. Help-lessness came over me in waves, even amid the rush of adrenaline that I could not express fast enough.

The trip down that ladder lasted an eternity.

My father had actually fallen thirty-five feet, landing on his back after colliding with a steel cable on the way down. He suffered broken vertebrae in his neck and shattered his kneecap. Although he was ex-pected to live, he died of internal injuries, secondary to medical malpractice, four days later, on January 4, 1975. That was not only the most traumatic day of my life, but also a key turning point in my growth.

My mother fell apart emotionally, as did my sis-ters, and I was called upon to become the "man of the house." I did this to the best of my ability, even though I, too, was traumatized and ill-prepared for such huge responsibilities at age twenty. Though I returned to college, resolving to excel in my career as my father had instructed me, I continued to work at least one more summer on another water tower, in spite of my new—and paralyzing—fear of heights. My father's previous insistence that I learn to burn and weld yielded high dividends in helping me pay my way through college, proving him prophetic in teaching me those timely and valuable skills.

My father's tragic death was simultaneously hor-rific and liberating—horrific because he had been my hero, but liberating because he was no longer con-trolling and mistreating me. I suffered six months of identical, unrelenting nightmares, in which my fa-ther was alive again, and my initial reaction was to experience tears of joy upon his miraculous return to life. Then each dream would quickly transform into agony, since he was back in my life, beating me once again, both physically and emotionally, recreating my feelings of worthlessness and powerlessness. Instead of being happy for his renewed life, it was as if my life was being sacrificed in a disempowering prison camp, to my despair and rage.

Acceptance ends the nightmares

After six months of this torment, I accepted the fact that my father had always cruelly dominated each of us. I accepted the truth that this was the side of him that I couldn't recognize consciously as long as I was memorializing him, clinging to an idealized image that I wished, in reality, he had been. When I reached that level of acceptance, my nightmares miraculously ended, teaching me a powerful psychological lesson:

The recognition and acceptance of any truth, no matter how disturbing, is both liberating and empowering.

After graduating college, I entered the University of Pittsburgh for five years of graduate studies in Educational Psychology, where I earned both MA and PhD degrees. I worked both as a Teaching Assistant and Teaching Fellow, and I continued to strive as a student to become my very best.

In 1979, two years before graduating from Pitt, I began to work full time at my first non-blue-collar job as a mental health clinician at a community mental health center children's outpatient department in Pittsburgh. While working there for almost five years, I concurrently earned both my PhD and

Psychologist license, and I attended a weekly Family Systems Therapy training seminar. My career spanned numerous professional roles with recurring growth opportunities and challenges until December 30, 2008, the day I registered my new enterprise, Piso and Associates, LLC. I finally became my own boss—completely free to stretch and grow, unfettered.

During the past six years, I have spent the majority of my professional time working as a consultant for health care, business, and educational clients across the country. My activities have also included research, book, and journal publications, and presentations at varied professional conferences.

My journey has included painful struggle, frustrating setbacks, recurring sacrifice, and continued learning with fervent passion. I have striven to assimilate all of these experiences—especially the most difficult ones—transforming them into personal assets and strengths. As in crafting a sword, the forging process has involved repeated beating of the metals and gradual tempering in hot fires before the final polishing would produce an effective tool.

While my abuse was quite real, I also received sufficient love from both parents and others to transform even my greatest suffering into sources of personal strength and compassion for others, especially for the disempowered of this world. I have come from a place of suffering, powerlessness, humiliation, depression, anxiety, loneliness, and a fragile sense of self-esteem, but I have attempted to mature and grow along the way.

My journey has opened doors to joy, confident strength, humility, graciousness, social connectedness, and a life of passionate, fulfilling service.

There is a profound Buddhist teaching that "What we resist persists," often accompanied by its companion wisdom, "Pain in life is inevitable, but suffering is an option." I thank God for my rich blessings, including my ability to accept the painful trials and turbulence that continue to work together for my refinement and tempering, so that suffering is now an option I have the power to reject. Most important, I have learned to love myself, unconditionally, thereby liberating me to create the beautifully soulful life I was intended to live from the beginning!

About the Author

Craig N. Piso, PhD is president of Piso and Associates, LLC, an organizational development consulting firm based in northeastern Pennsylvania. A licensed psychologist with over thirty-five years of training and experience, he has played roles in family systems clinical practice, corporate managed behavioral health, and health care/business/educational consulting. Specializations include: Leadership Development, Vision-Mission-Values Development, Team-Building, Cultural Transformation and Organizational Health/Effectiveness, Health

Coaching, Board Functionality and Partner Conflict Resolution, Physician Interpersonal Behavior, and Strategic Planning. Raised in Pittsburgh, Pennsylvania, Piso graduated Summa Cum Laude in Psychology from Grove City College, and earned MA and PhD degrees in Educational Psychology at the University of Pittsburgh.

Balboa Press published Craig Piso's first book, *Healthy Power—Pathways to Success in Work, Love and Life* in December, 2012, about which Wayne Dyer had this to say: "A stellar job, Craig: a well written, well organized and eminently readable book. I recommend it enthusiastically."

He and his wife, Theresa, reside in Wilkes-Barre, Pennsylvania. His website is PisoAndAssociates.com.

The Power I Earned by Losing Control

Martin Plowman

Italy, 2005.

As I lay flat on the paramedic's stretcher, fighting for air, I felt something I had never felt before.

The fear of dying.

Amazing, since moments before I had just experienced the biggest crash of my young racing career, losing control of my go kart on a wet track, slamming violently into the catch fencing at 70 mph.

I'd never before had a fear of dying, not even then, even though I had just been thrown out of my racing kart on impact, making full contact with the fence before flopping down into my seat, numb.

Time froze. There was only silence.

Then the pain washed over my body. I had never felt pain like this before, but worse than the pain was the fact that I couldn't breathe. I was fighting it, but my airwaves had closed so tightly I was completely unable to take in any air.

The paramedics were quick to the scene. They first removed my helmet. Then they carefully lifted me, still fighting for air, out of the kart and onto the stretcher, wary of possible spinal injuries. I had been badly winded in crashes before, and usually my breathing relaxed and returned to normal in under a minute. But I could tell something wasn't quite right this time, during this longest minute of my life. I started to black out, and to prevent that I slowly started to take short, wispy breaths of air, just enough to keep me conscious.

Suddenly my focus and attention had shifted from winning a race to winning the next second of my life.

This all happened at Italy's highly regarded 2,000-seat Lonato Kart track during the first round of the 2005 Italian Open Championship. I wasn't fluent in Italian, which meant that most of what the paramedics were saying was the equivalent of white noise during my journey to the hospital. As we were pulling up to the emergency entrance, Dino, my team manager, noticed my lips start to turn a shade of blue. This normally very confident guy was now very worried. I, on the other hand, was focused purely on the massive pain in my back and my inability to take anything but tiny, forced baby breaths.

I tried to stay relaxed, when really I was panicking. There it was, that unfamiliar fear of death.

Panicked voices on high alert
As the paramedics unloaded me from the ambulance, I remember the ceiling lights flashing by, doctors and nurses on either side of me as they wheeled me to an x-ray room. To this day I have no idea what the hospital looked like, but I could probably draw you a ceiling map. I had a full body x-ray, and then was wheeled back to another new room with a new set of faces I hadn't seen before.

One of the nurses sat me upright in the bed as the hospital team began to cut away at my torn-up suit. Underneath my race suit was my rib protector. In the mirror I could see the doctors carefully removing it, at which point blood gushed out against the wall behind me. Panic crept into the voices of everybody around me, and there was a flurry of urgent activity.

During the impact I had sustained a life-threatening puncture wound, piercing my right lung, missing my spine by less than an inch. Since this would remained undetected by the track doctors for over twenty-five minutes, I was close to being full of blood, and therefore close to suffocation. Corridor lights flickered by, and there was the sound of caster wheels clicking and the voice of an Italian doctor on high alert, a voice with the urgency of an Army drill instructor.

Up to this point I had felt nothing but numbness from the extreme pain. Everything was just happening around me, without me. Yet, as we hurried down the hallway, here was that unfamiliar fear again. Inside the operating theatre, I was laid out on my side. An English-speaking doctor leaned in to tell me that there wasn't enough time for a full anesthetic, that they would work with a local anesthetic and "not to worry." It was then that the helplessness of my situation hit me. Here I was, at the mercy of other people trying to save my life. My emotions went from fear to a combination of shock and fear.

So, is this really it?

This is not how it was supposed to be!

This is not part of my plan.

As the anesthetic started to wear off, the pain returned, creeping like a jagged dagger down my back. My heart rate started to rise rapidly, which didn't go unnoticed by the doctors, who gave me another shot of anesthetics. Straightaway my heart rate dropped. With a sheet over my head, I was semi-aware of my surroundings, in a drug-induced haze, my ears tuned to the sound of the heart-rate monitor. I heard the monitor's beep grow slower and slower, until the silences between beeps introduced a nervous wait, while I wondered if my heart might stop altogether.

A surreal moment's very real prayer

During that surreal moment is when I remember saying a prayer: *"God, I don't know if you can hear me, but I really need your help right now.* I don't know what you have planned for me, but all I ask right now is for strength and calmness."

Now, I am by no means a devoted religious person. Do I believe in God? Yes. Do I believe in a life after death? I would certainly like to think there will be one. Either way, no matter what a person's religion, I believe there is a Higher Power. There *has to be,* or what is this whole life worth anyway, if it is all for nothing? Otherwise, when the candle burns up, it's just darkness.

As I lay there thinking about the prayer I had just uttered, I realized that something big had happened:

I had just accepted my situation.

I had finally realized that I was not in control of "my plan," and "how it was supposed to be" was up to somebody else altogether. For the first time since arriving at the hospital, I felt serenely calm, despite the frantic work happening around me. I still didn't know if I was going to die, I was still fighting to breathe, and I was still in a ton of pain as the anesthetic wore off for a second time. But I felt at peace, at an extraordinary time to feel at peace.

Realizing I had no control over what lay ahead, I learned right there and then to trust in God.

The power of prayer was very real for me that day. It's hard to explain it, unless you have been in a similar situation, and it's even harder to prove any of it. But all I can say is that I felt all of the fear and shock fade away as a calmness descended on me, I became as serene as if I were just kicking back at home watching television. I can say to the skeptics and non-believers—at the very least, if you give it a try, the worst that may happen is you'll find yourself talking to yourself on a hospital bed.

Same corner, same deadly speed

Sometimes in life we get so caught up in our own plans, in what we want to happen, only to see our trains get derailed once in a while by outside occurrences. Something will hit us so hard, the message has to be that we are supposed to go in a different direction.

More times than not, if we trust this unexpected journey we've been sidetracked to, things work out surprisingly better than we could have hoped, even if they just don't seem to be working out "the way they are supposed to."

Obviously, I made it out alive and made a full recovery, since I'm writing this story right now! Several months later, once I was fully recovered, my team manager, Dino, took me back to the same track where I had my accident. He gave me strict instructions: to go flat out, right at the corner where I had crashed by lap three. Either that, or he would drive home and I would never race again. It was his way of testing how much the accident had affected me mentally. He wanted to see if I was 100%.

I took the challenge. Whether I was brave or just plain dumb, by the start of lap two I was already driving flat out through turn one, just to prove a point to Dino and to myself! Despite coming face to face with my own destiny just a few months earlier, I found that I was no longer scared of dying. It's not that I became reckless, or somehow even felt invincible. The truth is I believe there is a higher plan for all of us, so I just resigned myself to the fact that fear of dying was futile, as we don't really have a say about when we will go, anyway.

As I write this, it's been over ten years since I had my accident. Looking back, it's easy to see how this one accident shaped who I am and how I live my life today. I no longer live in fear. If anything, the accident galvanized my desire to "live life fuller."

I was very blessed to be able to return to full health and resume my pursuit of a career in motor sports. Ten years on from my accident, I will take the green flag in my very first 24 Hours of Le Mans, the world-famous pinnacle of Endurance Sports Car racing.

My dream job also happens to be a very dangerous job, and I have known what it is like to lose a good friend or two in this business. The truth is, to quit doing something that you have dedicated your heart and whole life to, simply for fear of dying, is to die a slow, empty life.

Every day that I get to sit in my race car is a blessing. What the accident taught me, more than anything, is that nothing lasts forever and everything you love can be taken away from you just as quickly as it is given.

If you can take just one thing away from my story, it would be this: *Don't fear fear.* Letting go of fear will help you enjoy your life in a more fulfilling way. And finally... don't be afraid to say a prayer. Do it alone by yourself, if you like.

As my mom always used to say "You never get, if you never ask."

About the Author

This is the first time Martin Plowman has told his dramatic story. Already one of the world's leading race car drivers, 2014 was Plowey's rookie year in the Indianapolis 500. Plowman was born in Burton upon Trent, Staffordshire, England, in 1987, a champion from the first time he stepped into a racing kart at the age of eight. He took First Place in his class of LMPZ in the 24 Hour LeMans, thought to be the most difficult and prestigious race in the world. Plowman, who moved to Indianapolis in 2009, hopes to win the Borg Warner Trophy one day. His wins are many and impressive, and can be found on his website, Martin-Plowman.com. Follow him on Twitter @Plowey.

Breaking Open

Deanna Stull

Today I stand balanced on the line between life and death.
Not yet steady, I am poised between the past and the future, between devastation and possibility. It is a tight-rope dance. I teeter, one foot tentatively placed in front of another, a few steps forward, a few back, arms stretched into the air.
Today this line where sorrow and joy intersect feels more delineated than it has in quite some time. This line is where one finds the truth that with immense pain, there is always undeniable beauty.

The sky is the brightest blue. The sun pierces the trees, dappled by the leaves as they sway in the breeze. The garden is so alive with the green of early summer. Birds sing in a chaotic choir, celebrating life as I waver between tears and a peaceful calm, between gratitude and deep, intense sorrow.

It is the anniversary of Blake's diagnosis. Today marks four years since leukemia changed our lives, and a year and a half since Blake's death. Today also marks the day I truly started living life fully and completely. I've grown surprisingly comfortable walking this line, and more and more grateful every day for my skill at this precarious balancing act.

Above all else, I am grateful that I met Blake. If given the chance to walk hand in hand with him on his final journey again, I would.

I remember the day we met as if it were yesterday. He walked into the Morning Glory Café, and I knew.

He sat down and we started talking and I knew I had found my partner, my best friend and my true love.

Our journey together offered learning far beyond what I considered possible with either lover or friend. It was a lesson I had avoided receiving for most of my life, one that challenged the very fabric of my being, but one that ultimately allowed me to be present *as myself* for the first time, ever.

When you become a caregiver for a cancer patient, everything in your life changes.

Everything.

The comfort of strangers

Blake was so sick at the time of his diagnosis that he was given last rites while he was still in the ER; they did not expect him to make it to the ICU. I did the best I could to stay strong as the doctors came and went and his condition continually worsened, but whenever I'd take a few steps out into the hallway, I would break down completely. It was the first time I'd ever allowed myself such vulnerability in public. Complete strangers would stop to comfort me as I stood in the hallway, sobbing, devastated. In a stranger's embrace my life began to change.

People prepare you for the heartbreak of cancer and loss, but they don't often talk about the positive experience that can accompany it, as if acknowledging the good would deny the painful reality. But I discovered that finding the positive in incredibly difficult moments allows you to fully live your life, regardless of the challenge presented.

Blake's leukemia required intense treatment: five-day inpatient chemotherapy for months, followed by more intensive chemotherapy and full-body radiation, which prepared him for a stem cell transplant. He developed Graft Versus Host Disease (GVHD) and several active viruses. The treatment left him wheelchair bound. And yet he recovered fully.

We had amazing fun, creating wonderful memories, even while cancer and its treatments dominated our lives. We never stopped loving life, we went on day trips, we went to the beach. We took advantage of the times Blake felt well, and went out into the world to live.

While in remission, Blake was diagnosed with a second leukemia, a rare but indolent cancer that required immuno-suppressants. He bounced back and was on the road to recovery once again. Unfortunately, the medication left Blake very susceptible to infection, and he developed pneumonia. But he recovered once again, and we were able to go on vacation to the White Mountains of New Hampshire for a week when cancer no longer existed, and life felt normal again.

It was brief. The pneumonia returned, and with it, GVHD, which lead to another hospitalization. Despite a few more setbacks, including some heart issues, Blake was about to be released from the hospital when he suddenly required surgery for appendicitis. After his recovery and a few brief days at home, an ambulance took him for his final ride to the hospital.

Heartbroken peace

It seems so strange to write it all out like this in one neat paragraph, because what Blake endured was so intense that even supporting him in it proved to be incredibly challenging. Though I was utterly heartbroken when he took his last breath, I felt a deep sense of peace in knowing that he would no longer endure any of that terrible pain again.

Blake's last hospitalization was short. He went downhill quickly. On Friday, we were told it was another bump in the road, and on Sunday I walked in to find him on a respirator, just barely able to communicate. He said only a few things to me that day, most of which were very private, but two things I will share with you. "I love you, and I am proud of you," and "I want the respirator removed." He wasn't able to speak; he was barely able to whisper and mouth the words. I tried to ignore the last sentence, so he said it again. "I want the respirator removed." I looked him in the eye and asked, "Are you sure you no longer want to fight?" "I am sure," he said. My next question seems so odd to me now, "Are you finished?" He nodded his head and whispered.

"I am done."

Two-and-a-half years of fighting ended in less than twenty-four hours. The respirator was removed in the late afternoon of October 21, and on October 22, 2012, two days before my birthday, Blake took his last breath.

On the day of his death, I broke wide open.

I struggled to maintain my tenuous grip on control. Surrounded by family intent on helping Blake and me through this, I held so much in because I thought they could not handle it.

As the day unfolded, and our heartbreak grew, I contracted even deeper inside of myself. Not wanting them to see my weakness, I withdrew, until it became physically painful for me to stay self-contained.

My heart hurt. It was hard to breathe. I thought I was having a heart attack. And even then, I told no one. Instead, I bought some aspirin and quietly took it, never sharing what was happening. Even with the possibility of a heart attack, I refused to let go of control until the enormity of change hit me squarely in the face.

Blake's fight with leukemia taught me difficult lessons I would never forget. But Blake's approaching death was what truly brought me to my knees. It was while I was on my knees that things began to change even more.

Sitting vigil, struggling with the fact that his letting go was not as easy for him as I had hoped, I hid myself and my grief behind the curtains in the corner of his ICU room.

A private plea to all the world
There, hidden away, I reached out for support the only way I could think of in that moment. I found myself very quietly typing, "I need help, help me be

strong" on my computer.

Then I hit POST.

So began my personal journey of loss, sharing my grief... on Facebook.

I had no choice but to let go. I had to let go of my expectations of what I wanted, had to let go of my need for him to continue fighting.

I had to let go of my desire to fix everything and everyone. I had to let go of my need to look like I had it all together. I had to let go of handling everything all on my own.

I had to let go of not wanting to ask for help. I had to let go of keeping control. I had to let go of hiding my emotions. I had to let go of fear.

I had to let go of Blake.

In letting go, I found myself. The messiness, pain and emotion of losing Blake left me no other alternative but to let go of pretense, doubt, and fear, and it all began the moment I posted my need for help on Facebook.

That's when my intensely private grief took on the most public face, as I silently cried out for help online, there behind the ICU curtain. That privately public moment marked an enormous change for me, rippling across all areas of my life.

I broke wide open on social media, for all the world to see.

Before Blake's diagnosis, I always successfully avoided sickness and its ramifications—caregiving, death, and funerals—at all cost. I did well holding it all together, but I feared the possibility of people seeing how emotional I was, how deeply I felt loss and pain. I thought showing vulnerability meant I was weak, and I never wanted to show weakness.

Standing up for Blake

But typing my cry for help and posting it on Facebook continued the process of significant change that started, the day of Blake's diagnosis, in the arms of a stranger who stopped to console me as I wept. It was not an immediate change; it was the beginning of a journey that continued through the morning of Blake's memorial service, when I insisted I would write a eulogy, but that I would not read it. Vulnerability was not an easy path for me.

The morning of the memorial, I woke up to a beautiful fall day. I sat up in bed, knowing I would be the one to speak, after all. So I did, stepping out onto that tightrope, finding my balance and my footing. I stood up in front of all those mourning his loss and said all the things Blake would have wanted them to know. Together, we laughed, cried, and then laughed again, remembering the important things, the things you shouldn't need cancer and death to teach you.

I had found myself, but this was the most open, courageous, and truthful version of myself I've ever been. I no longer hid from pain and heartbreak. Instead, I embraced it as part of a life well lived.

What Blake gave me was the ability to break wide open, to share my broken, yet beautiful pieces with the world so others could find solace in my journey.

These days I honor my life, and our life together by living my emotions as I am feeling them, raw and unfiltered, which allows me to let go in a peaceful and authentic way. Intermixed with all the harshness, challenges, and incredibly difficult moments of Blake's last days, there was always life, breathtaking, miraculous, generous life. Unbelievable sunrises, with wild reds, vibrant oranges and bright yellows still danced across the bay in the morning. The smell of the salty ocean air still cradled me in its fragrant, humid arms.

We were still the two who met each other those many years ago in that café in Philadelphia. As hard as cancer was, it could not stop our laughter from breaking through the sound of the hospital's monitoring equipment, drawing the nurses into Blake's room for stories and silliness. We laughed during the last few days of Blake's life. We cried, yes. We embraced what was, yes. And we walked together, hand in hand, into his last days on earth, honoring life and its beautiful contradictions.

We kept hold of all that was important to us and, through the darkest hours, the brilliance of life held us gently, beckoning us to come back into the light that is always there.

I found this in Blake's final notebook:
"When the journey is meant to be taken, choosing the path is not so difficult… When the journey is meant to be taken, the road you're on is always the most scenic."

About the Author

Above all else, Deanna Stull, PCC, is here to create a more courageous and inspired world. In service to her destiny, she is a storyteller, best-selling author (*Speaking Your Truth, Courageous Stories from Inspiring Women - Volume Three*), speaker, professional coach, and trainer. She is an ICF Certified Professional Coach and Higher Ground Leadership Pathfinder, advancing the field of coaching as the CXO of CoachVille, one of the largest, most comprehensive and most progressive coach training schools in the world. Deanna is a rebel with a cause who coaches and inspires individuals, businesses, and organizations to become leaders in the pursuit of human greatness so they can change the world. She lives in the beautiful farmlands of Pennsylvania with her inspired and loving dog, Pippin.

You can visit Deanna at DeannaStull.com

Deanna Stull's Lessons Learned from

Love and Loss

1. Trust me, beauty dwells in the dark recesses and in the emptiness as well. Opening your heart wider helps you to see this.

2. Amazing memories will be more significant to you in the end than anything else. Spend your days creating as many as you can.

3. When asked, people will step up to help in unimaginable ways. And just when you think they've given all they possibly can, wait. There will be more.

4. The most painful times of your life often produce the most breathtaking moments of pure and simple truth.

5. People will express their opinions, telling you how to be and what to do, because they love you and are fearful. Remember the first part—they love you. Let go of the rest.

6. This is the moment to begin making whatever changes you need to fully live out your purpose, right now. Not "... when this or that is done..." or "I need to, before..." The comfort zone is no place for you. There is no better time than now to start anew.

7. Go ahead, make mistakes, take chances that might not pan out. Do that often. The most successful people experience the most spectacular crashes and the craziest, most awkward moments. Join them.

8. When life is challenging, and it will be, you will not just survive, you will thrive if you've got a

massive support system behind you. Spend more time with those you love, it will make all the difference.

9. You are not playing enough. Play adds joy, creativity, resilience, wonder, and energy to our lives. Blake and I brought the spirit of play even to some of the most critical moments of his leukemia treatment, including our discussions about the big "What Ifs." I am eternally grateful that we did. When you play, you are more alive. Play!

10. Spend the majority of your time here doing *things you'd like to be known for*, instead of things that are easy to cross off a list.

11. You are strong, resilient, and beautiful. Whenever you feel "less than," read this and be reminded.

Marilyn Gansel, PsyD, is a sports psychologist, life coach, and educator in Kent, Connecticut. Dr. Gansel is available for workshops and seminars as well as one-on-one or group coaching by phone or in person. She can be reached at DrM@DrMLifeCoach.com. Visit DrMLifeCoach.weebly.com.

Patricia G. Horan is a veteran editor, with experience at Crown/Random House books, Times Mirror and Rupert Murdoch magazines and many others. Among the many book publishers she has written or edited titles for are Crown, Time-Life Books, Viking and Penguin/Tarcher. She and her Round House Press are based in Asheville, North Carolina. Info@ TheRoundHousePress.com.

CPSIA information can be obtained
at www.ICGtesting.com
Printed in the USA
FFOW02n0558251117
43700201-42558FF